TWRIO

Editors

Carol and Robert Pugh

TOWY PUBLISHING

© The individual contributors 2001

First published: 2001

Published by
Towy Publishing
P.O. Box 24, Carmarthen, SA31 1YS
Telephone: (01267) 236569.

ISBN 0 9525790 22

Typeset and printed in Wales by
Dinefwr Press, Rawlings Road, Llandybïe,
Carmarthenshire, SA18 3YD.

CONTENTS

THANKS

We thank, not only the contributors for their writing and photographs, but also John Watkin (producer), Geraint Lewis (director) and Shân Crofft of Pedol Television, the Staff of Carmarthen Museum, the National Museum of Wales, Neil and Glynda Speed, John Fry (photographer), and Luned Whelan of Hughes (S4C) Publishing.

WELSH POTTERY

Robert Pugh

THIS IS A BRIEF SURVEY of the three main factories of South
Wales – The Cambrian Pottery at Swansea, its near neighbour
The Glamorgan Pottery and the South Wales Pottery, usually
referred to as 'Llanelly' and three smaller factories that operated in
the Swansea area.

The story of the Welsh commercial potteries began on a site on
the river Tawe (near what is now Swansea railway station) in 1764,
and ended on the recently redeveloped old gasworks site at the top
of Market Street, Llanelli, in 1922. In the intervening hundred and
fifty years much everyday pottery was produced and, from time to
time, things that were quite extraordinary, making the collecting of
our native products such a pleasure.

THE CAMBRIAN POTTERY, SWANSEA, 1764-1870

The Swansea Pottery, which soon became known as The Cambrian
Pottery, was founded by William Coles as a part of his extensive
business empire. He died within fifteen years of the inception leaving it to his three sons, but it was his youngest son John who was
most involved and who, in 1790, entered into partnership with his
manager, George Haynes. Haynes was already the most important
figure in the life of the Cambrian during the years which we have
come to recognise as its golden period.

In 1802 William Dillwyn, a Quaker of Welsh decent who had been
born in the USA, bought a majority share in the Pottery for his son

Lewis Weston Dillwyn. George Haynes retained his own interest but this was considerably smaller than that of his young partner. This situation seems to have worked well for some eight years, but finally a falling out came and Haynes left the pottery in 1810.

The dispute between Haynes, who it should be remembered was an important man in Swansea and West Wales business and Banking circles, and young Dillwyn was of a serious nature. It resulted in litigation and caused Haynes, through intermediaries, to start up a rival pottery, The Glamorgan Pottery, on a site next door to the Cambrian.

In 1817 Dillwyn retired from the day to day running of the pottery and granted a lease to his managers T. & J. Bevington, who took Haynes back as a partner. This period was not a success and few innovative designs were produced. 1824 saw L. W. Dillwyn taking back control and he ran the pottery until 1831 when he was succeeded by his second son, Lewis Llewellyn Dillwyn.

L. Ll. Dillwyn was the driving force behind the pottery right through until 1850 when he retired. A lease on the pottery was then granted to his manager David Evans and to John Glasson who was a West Country traveller for the Cambrian's rival, the Llanelli based, South Wales Pottery. Glasson died in 1852 but the pottery continued to be known as Evans and Glasson until David Evans himself retired in 1862, handing over the business to his son. After this the business was called D. J. Evans and Co until its closure in 1870 when L. Ll. Dillwyn arranged to sell the headlease of the property for other purposes.

The type of wares produced during the early period fall into three main categories.

Very early pieces are now only rarely found. These items were either saltglaze or ordinary glaze on simple objects. Saltglaze is a method of glazing achieved very simply by throwing salt into the firing. The result is an all over glaze with a slightly rough 'orange peel' texture. The only method of decoration on any of these very early pieces is incised scratch decoration, simply done by hand and

Three 'standard' Swansea blue and white patterns.
Left to right: Minoptoris; Elephant Rocks; Ladies of Llangollen.

often filled with blue colour. Thus it is usually referred to by collectors as 'scratch blue'.

In about 1790, one **Thomas Rothwell** came to work in Swansea. He was a copper-plate engraver of the very highest skill and he was responsible for the extremely fine quality blue and white transfer ware produced at the pottery. Amongst his most famous patterns are the Swansea 'Elephant' pattern and the 'mock willow' pattern (sometimes with moth border), that is usually referred to as the 'Longbridge' pattern. The skill of the copper-plate engraver is not to be overlooked. Often people talk of hand painting as the finest possible type of decoration and indeed at its very best it was. However, the achievement of the man who can engrave up to twenty different metal plates, each with an identical pattern of different size, is considerable.

The next important step was the introduction of creamware to Swansea. This fine cream coloured earthenware had been invented by Wedgwood and named Queensware by him after interest had

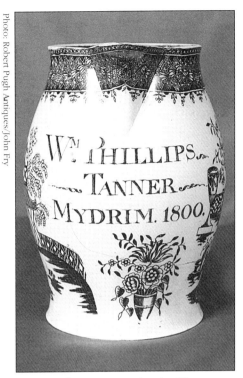

Photo: Robert Pugh Antiques/John Fry

A Cambrian Pottery jug by Thomas
Rothwell. Meidrim ('Mydrim') is
a village near Carmarthen.

been shown by the Royal family. The Swansea creamware was every bit as good as that of their rival and is often found exquisitely decorated. The main decorator at Swansea throughout this period was **Thomas Pardoe** who is perhaps best known for his wonderful botanical pieces, after prints by Curtis. Young Dillwyn was a keen botanist and was clearly the influence behind this form of decoration. Pardoe also decorated in other styles, particularly in iron red and cobalt blue.

The other main decorator, whose work is found very much less often than Pardoe, is **William Weston Young**. His main contribution to Welsh ceramics was in his involvement with Billingsly and Walker at Nantgarw, but as a painter of deceptively simple landscapes, butterflies and animals on creamware, Young has no rival.

The main products of the factory throughout this period were table wares, both transfer-printed and hand-painted. Only a limited number of purely decorative items were made and these include elaborate figures of Anthony and Cleopatra, modelled by George Bently, a famous modeller, brought to Swansea by Haynes.

The quality of Swansea Pottery during this, pre-1810 period, both in terms of the pottery itself and its decoration, was second to none.

During the 1810-1850 period, under the stewardship of the Dillwyn family, and briefly under the Bevingtons, the products of the factory were also to a very high standard. The Bevington period was not a success but the operation could be seen to be running on more commercial lines under the Dillwyns.

This period offers the richest field for collectors with a wide range of quality items to choose from. In the main the products were transfer-printed wares. Obviously some patterns were more popular than others, while some were clearly made only for brief periods or only in very small quantities for reasons now unknown to us. The result is that those surviving vary considerably in availability. The commonest is ordinary 'Willow' pattern, while the rarest of all is 'Cheetah' a pattern which is known in only four or five examples. The skill of today's collector lies in the instinct to know whether to leave something alone in the hope that it will come up again, perhaps at a better price, or to strike while the iron is hot and grasp a once-in-a-lifetime opportunity!

Between the extremes of 'Willow' and 'Cheetah' are a huge range of differing transfer patterns. Some of the best known are 'Ladies with Baskets' usually found printed in black and interesting because the pattern fills the plate, without a border, 'Cows crossing a stream', 'Whampoa' and 'Lazulai', an all over pattern usually called a 'sheet' pattern.

Swansea Pottery. A Cambrian (c.1800) creamware dish with a sepia painting landscape.
A rare frog mug in Ottoman pattern (c.1830) and a creamware pierced border or ribbon plate.

During the 1830/50 period the cow creamers for which Swansea is well known were produced, along with the pierced border or 'ribbon' plates. West country and local views are also from this period, as are the various religious commemoratives for Wesley and James Teare.

Some hand painting also occurs but not of the quality found during the earlier period. However, pieces are sometimes found individually inscribed with names places and, most importantly, dates. Such items are always of particular interest to collectors.

The products of the pottery very gradually deteriorated during the first half of the nineteenth century and the quality of the first twenty five years was not repeated. Certainly, but very gradually, quality gave way to commercial considerations.

In the late 1840's Dillwyn made one last attempt at artistic achievement with the introduction of a reproduction of a series of Ancient Greek items copied by his wife from originals in the British Museum. This series, made from terracotta clay excavated from his brother's estate at Penllergaer, was known as and marked *Dillwyn's Etruscan Ware*.

A selection of 1830's Swansea Pottery.

Generally, the wares of the Evans and Glasson and D. J. Evans periods are of little quality and, beyond a few technical rarities, are not highly sought by collectors.

MARKS ON SWANSEA POTTERY

1783-1810   SWANSEA usually impressed but unusually in script Cambrian rare mark in script.

1802-1817   Impressed marks incorporating the name DILLWYN and/or SWANSEA.

1817-1824   (somewhat unusually) BEVINGTON & CO.

1824-1850   as 1802-1817 and Cymro Stone China in a raised cartouche.

1850-1870   Various marks impressed and printed incorporating the name Evans and Glasson or D. J. Evans.

THE GLAMORGAN POTTERY, 1813-1839

The disagreement between Lewis Llewellyn Dillwyn and George Haynes had resulted in Haynes leaving the Cambrian Pottery where he had been the leading light for two decades. Under the guise of his son-in-law and two other partners, he built a new pottery on a site close to the Cambrian and opened in competition.

The products of the Glamorgan Pottery were similar in many ways to those of their older rival and very much of a high quality commercial nature. The factory is particularly renowned for the quality of its transfer printing with some of its patterns, notably 'The

Ladies of Llangollen', being of better standard than that produced by the Cambrian.

Many shapes similar to those used by the Cambrian are employed and it is the standard, most common, shaped jug that the factory made that we have come to call 'Glamorgan' shape, even when used by either of the other Welsh factories. This shape is identical to that used in both Llanelly and Cambrian, the difference lies only on the handle, each factory having a handle shape unique to that factory.

Amongst items familiar to Cambrian collectors will be pierced-edge plates and cow creamers. These latter, very close in shape to their neighbours, were often transfer printed at the Glamorgan Pottery and it is now these transfer-printed examples that are the most sought after of Welsh cows.

The factory ran until 1839. George Haynes had died in 1830 and the last few years of the pottery's life were not easy financially. In 1837 Dillwyn agreed to purchase the business to close it down. Its influence was to continue however, because many skilled workmen and ideas transferred to the new pottery being created by William Chambers Jnr., ten miles down the coast at Llanelli.

MARKS ON GLAMORGAN POTTERY

A small variety of impressed and transferred marks were used all incorporating the names or initials of the partners Baker Bevan and Irwin (*BB&I*).

LLANELLY POTTERY
or THE SOUTH WALES POTTERY AT LLANELLY

The South Wales Pottery was commenced in 1839 by William Chambers Jnr., the son of the local lord of the manor at Llanelli and a prominent local businessman and magistrate in his own right. The factory was to survive for some eighty years and outlast the Cambrian Pottery by fifty.

Chambers had two big advantages in setting up his new business. Firstly, he was creating a new factory from scratch with all the advantages of the very latest equipment, and secondly he has a supply of first class and experienced labour on his doorstep as a result of Dillwyn's closure of the Glamorgan Pottery.

Chambers ran the South Wales Pottery for the first sixteen years of its life. In 1855 his father died and for complicated inheritance reasons he left Llanelli. The pottery business was then sold to Messrs Coombes and Holland. Coombes left the business very soon afterwards, leaving Holland as the proprietor until 1875. The factory was then closed for two years due to financial problems but was resurrected in 1877 by David Guest and his cousin Richard Dewsberry (David Guest having been a partner of Holland's for the latter part of his proprietorship). By 1906 both these partners had died leaving Richard Guest, David's son, as sole proprietor. In 1912 the business became a company but in 1922 was forced to close.

The products of the factory fall into three fairly easily defined periods:

During the period of William Chambers Jnr. the factory was a typical mid-Victorian factory of a Staffordshire type, but with a particularly wide variety of output. It is from this period that many of the great rarities emerge.

The day-to-day output consisted of dinner services, toilet wares and items for everyday living, usually produced in one of the more common patterns, Willow, Milan, Amherst Japan or Damask Boarder. However, many experiments were conducted and this results in such unusual items as the blue 'Stag' jugs, copper luster clock jugs and a wide range of rare shapes and bodies. Some patterns, too, are now much rarer than others particularly some of those used on the child's plates, so much a hallmark of the early period.

The middle period, that of William Holland is characterised by the high standard both of the 'body' (that is the pottery itself), and the transfer decoration. Sometimes the pottery bears an impressed mark 'ironstone' and this hard, heavy body is the perfect vehicle for high quality transfer ware. The variety of prints is not quite as great as the Chambers period but quality is foremost with the factory winning prizes in international competition with a pattern named 'Flora'.

It is one of the ironies of collecting Llanelly Pottery that the most sought-after period is the last one. By this time the quality of the actual pottery has deteriorated alarmingly, as indeed has the quality of the transfer wares. It was at this point that hand painting again become popular at Llanelli. The first of this hand painting was probably what we call Persian Rose, a very simplistic design of red green and blue flowers that certainly has a great charm but which was painted extremely quickly onto a coarse body with a minimum of skill involved. Certainly the level of expertise involved here was nowhere near as great as either the engraver of copper plates for transfer making, nor indeed the girl who would have applied the transfer paper to the pot. Sarah Roberts' famous Llanelly 'cockerel' plates were probably not in production until well into the twentieth century and those dated examples we know of are between 1910 and the first war.

By this time a small concern like Llanelly pottery had huge and insurmountable opposition from Staffordshire and the writing was already on the wall very early in the century.

In 1908 one final burst of enthusiasm was generated by the arrival of Samuel Shufflebotham at Llanelly. He was a painter of flowers and fruit on a specially produced cream coloured body. This body was a good colour but of poor quality and his work has a charm without being particularly skilled. However, the combination seems to have a magic appeal to today's collectors for, despite its youth, his work now fetches as much, or more, than any other Welsh Pottery. Ironically, there is little or no interest in his subsequent work in Devon.

Samuel Shufflebotham left Llanelli in 1915 and only a few years were to ebb away before the firing of the final kiln in 1922.

CALLANDS POTTERY, LANDORE, 1852-1856

Callands Pottery at Landore was a very-short lived venture that began in September, 1852. Its preliminary advertising stated that 'earthenware of every variety is manufactured'. James Hinkley, who had been Lewis Llewellyn Dillwyn's manager at the Cambrian Pottery, was the agent for Callands, which would have been a great benefit to them. However, times were not good for the pottery industry and Callands factory was offered for sale as early as mid-1853, before it was a year old. Another attempt to let the premises was made in 1855 and the following year it was let for an unrelated purpose.

The main pattern for which Callands is known is Syria and the factory is also known to have produced Willow pattern. However, very little marked Callands comes to light. Marked examples of 'Sirius' pattern are marked in transfer *Callands Swansea* above and below the pattern name. The Sirius copper plates were to end up at the South Wales Pottery at Llanelli where examples are found retaining the pattern mark with the words Callands Swansea scoured out on the copper plate.

THE DYVATTY STREET POTTERY
(Pleasant Vale Pottery) 1843-1892

Very little is known about this pottery despite it comparatively long life. It would appear to have been started in about 1843 by one

William Mead, a potter from Bovey Tracey, who came to Swansea to work at the Cambrian, and continued until 1892.

It is probable that the main products of this pottery were industrial and simple red earthenware items for domestic use. It certainly seems unlikely that any form of decoration as such was attempted. Game-jugs, elaborately moulded with hares and other game and glazed in a thick, dark brown glaze (usually referred to as Rockingham glaze), have always been attributed to this factory but it now seems unlikely that they were made there. Certainly, game-jugs of the type believed to be Dyfatty were made at Llanelli (and marked SOUTH WALES POTTERY), and presumably in Staffordshire.

No marked items have been recorded.

YNYSMEUDDWY POTTERY, 1845-1875

The pottery at Ynysmeudwy came into being in 1845 when it was opened as a brickworks by two brothers Michael Martyn Williams and William Williams. By 1849, it had taken on the character of a traditional Victorian pottery making a variety of table wares, jugs and childs' plates. William Williams carried on alone from 1856 to 1859 and was then, in turn, superseded by Charles Williams, another brother, for just one year.

From 1860 until 1869 the factory was owned by Griffith Lewis and John Morgan owners of the Primrose Colliery at Pontardawe. In 1869 John Morgan died and in 1871 Griffith Lewis sold out to W. T. Holland, the owner of Llanelly Pottery. Holland then removed such plant as was of use to him to Llanelli, and continued to run Ynysmeudwy as a manufactory of bricks, chimney pots, garden ornaments and pipes etc. During this short period, up to 1875 when the Llanelly pottery was forced to close briefly, some of the Ynysmeudwy patterns and shapes were also in use at Llanelly.

The body of Ynysmeudwy pots, while not comparable to that of the early Cambrian wares, was of reasonable quality, and the standard

A rare Ynysmeudwy Pottery plate.
Sponged decoration.

of some of the transfer ware was very high. Many of the patterns employed at this factory were taken over by William Holland and used at Llanelly.

This question of the overlap between Llanelly and Ynysmeudwy does seem to have caused difficulties for students of Welsh pottery for some time. The answer seems to be that Holland produced no pottery of a domestic, decorated, type at Ynysmeudwy, but did make use of the Ynysmeudwy moulds and patterns in Llanelli. Some patterns became standard to Llanelly, but are more unusual than the established Llanelly patterns, and it may be that they were made as replacements only.

Ynysmeudwy has always been noted for its childs' plates which come in a wide variety of patterns. 'Red Riding Hood', 'Women Feeding Fowls', 'Boy Driving Geese', 'A Dead Bee Maketh No Honey' are all recorded in the collection of the National Museum of

Wales, and Noel Riley in her excellent book on childrens' pottery records a man minding turkeys and 'This Boy I Think Looks Very Grand Driving Out His Four in Hand'.

In common with the other Welsh Potteries, Ynysmeudwy produced Mocha ware. This was made almost entirely for the pub trade and is found in the form of mugs and jugs. As ever, Mocha ware is unmarked and difficult to identify accurately.

There was also some hand-decoration in the latter period at Ynysmeudwy, and much that has been found on the site is similar, but not identical, to Llanelly Persian Rose, which it predates by some years. Sponge decorated items were also made there.

MARKS

Marks on Ynysmeudwy pottery include transfer pattern marks including the name Williams or just the initials WW, and also impressed marks YNYSMEUDWY POTTERY; YNYSMEUDWY POTTERY SWANSEA VALE and YMP. Latterly, under Lewis and Morgan, the products were completely unmarked.

FURTHER READING

E. Morton Nance   *The Pottery and Porcelain of Swansea and Nantgarw*, Batsford 1942 (now available in facsimile reprint).

Sotheby's   The Catalogue of the Sir Leslie Joseph Collection.

Dilys Jenkins   Llanelly Pottery, DEB Books, 1968.

Gareth Hughes   *Llanelly Pottery*, Llanelli Borough Council,
& Robert Pugh   1990.

Robert Pugh   *Welsh Pottery – A Towy Guide.* Towy
                       Publishing, 1995.

Helen Hallesey   *The Glamorgan Pottery at Swansea*, Gomer
                       Press, 1995.

Lynn Bebb   *Welsh Pottery.* Shire Publications.

PUBLIC COLLECTIONS OF WELSH POTTERY

The National Museum of Wales, Cathays Park, Cardiff.
The Sir Leslie Joseph Gallery houses the world's finest collection
of Welsh ceramics.

Swansea Museum, formerly The Royal Institution of South Wales.

The Glynn Vivian Art Gallery, Alexandra Road, Swansea.

The Carmarthenshire County Council, The Mansion House
(Bryncaerau), Parc Howard, Llanelli (Llanelly Pottery only, but a
definitive collection).

Carmarthen Museum, The Old Bishop's Palace, Abergwili, near
Carmarthen.

COMMEMORATIVE POTTERY
IN THE SOUTH WALES FACTORIES

Robert Pugh

COMMEMORATIVE CERAMICS have always been a delight to collectors. This probably stems from childhood memories of being given mugs to commemorate public, usually Royal, events and adding them to the family collection of such things.

Generally speaking it is the earlier items that are most sought and while there are many examples of individually desirable pieces from the twentieth century, the death of Prince Albert is usually considered to be the last Royal event for which all serious commemoratives are desirable. Thereafter each event had many mass produced items not quite so worthy of the collector's attention. However, as time goes by the demand for later commemoratives grows.

Photo: Robert Pugh Antiques/John Fry

Swansea Pottery mug commemorating John Jones the M.P. for Carmarthen.

As well as Royal occasions, political events and personalities are also subject to the potters work. Many of these items, being of limited appeal originally, are now very rare indeed. Most nineteenth century potteries produced commemoratives of one sort or another and the Welsh factories were no exception.

The certain identification of transfer-decorated items made at the

Cambrian Pottery in the early years, that is pre-1811, is notoriously difficult. There are a number of commemorative items from this period that have, from time to time, been attributed to Swansea. However, in the absence of greater knowledge, we are restricting our list of Swansea commemoratives to items that we are certain 'beyond reasonable doubt' can be ascribed to the factory.

The first recorded Swansea commemorative is not, in fact, a transfer-decorated item but a jug, hand-decorated in cobalt blue, and commissioned by Joseph Vaughn to commemorate the victory of Admiral Rodney over the Dutch and Spanish fleets at St Eustabus in the West Indies. Joseph Vaughn's relation, Sir John Vaughn, fought with Rodney. The jug, now in the collection of the National Museum of Wales, is inscribed, *John Vaughn Melingriffey. Success to Admiral Rodney And His Majesty's Navy 1781.*

In 1793, the King and Queen of France were executed in Paris. A small number of pearl-ware mugs are recorded, showing the profiles of the King and Queen of France and the King and Queen of England disguised in the pattern. The mugs are inscribed, *A New Puzzle of PORTRAITS. Striking Likenesses of the King and Queen of England and the late King and Queen of France.*

Nelson is known to have visited the Cambrian Pottery with the Hamiltons in 1802. Much was made of this visit and Nelson ordered pottery for himself, decorated by Thomas Pardoe. It seems likely, then, that the Pottery would have commemorated some of Nelson's victories and his death in 1805, but which, if any, of the Nelson commemorative items were made at Swansea is not known. However, a large mug bearing a portrait of Nelson is certainly Swansea-painted by Thomas Pardoe.

Perhaps the finest Cambrian commemoratives of all are the Wellington jugs. These are fully marked with transfer marks, unique to them, *Dillwyn and Co Swansea* in a circle. The main transfer shows Wellington surrounded by a wreath of laurel leaves and on one side Britannia trampling a French flag and on the other side a figure representing Victory. The inside rim of the jug lists the great man's battle honours. While the jugs are usually inscribed *'Wellington'*, sometimes they bear the words *'Marquis Wellington'*, a title he held briefly in 1813 before being elevated to his dukedom.

The best-known anti-Napoleon commemoratives are two variations of cartoons transfer printed on jugs by the Cambrian Pottery in 1814 from copper plates engraved by Brindley. Both depict groups of good British chaps, with speech balloons emerging from their mouths, uttering all sorts of anti-Napoleon slogans. These cartoons are found in three sizes, and either in black transfer on white ground with coloured enamelling, or in red transfer on a 'canary' yellow ground.

The Glamorgan Pottery was not to be left out of this patriotic enthusiasm and produced jugs showing a seven-horned beast rising from the sea and the words *Buonoparte The Monstrous beast.*

Two local political items were also made at about this time. The more unusual of these commemorates the victory of John Owen Esq in the election for Pembroke on October 30th, 1812. The other records the victory of John Jones, of Ystrad House, in the Parliamentary election for Carmarthen in 1824.

The Great Reform Act of 1832 was the next event to stir the potters of Swansea. It seems unlikely that the Cambrian Pottery produced Reform jugs but the Glamorgan produced a variety. They were in two shapes, a round pedestal jug and the standard (in this case the more rare) Glamorgan-shaped jug. The basic print shows portraits of Althorp, Grey, Russell and Brougham in oval medallions and the words *Royal Assent to the Reform Bill 7 June 1832*. All these jugs tend to be marked with the standard Glamorgan mark of BB&I in a cartouche.

Although not strictly commemorative, it is worth mentioning the rare Glamorgan Pottery jugs depicting Daniel O'Connell and Father Matthew. These are printed in black with the words *Dan'l O'Connell Esqre* and *The very Revd Father Matthew The Two Great Regenerators of Ireland.*

The coming to the throne of Queen Victoria in 1837 was an event that was, inexplicably, not much commemorated in ceramic terms, as one might think. Thus, the items made by the Cambrian Pottery are eagerly sought-after by collectors of both Welsh ceramics and commemorative items. Two different mugs were produced, both usually printed in purple. The smaller (2⅞ inches) simply shows a portrait of the Queen with the inscription QUEEN VICTORIA. The larger mug, which has an elaborate 'crested' handle, bears a similar portrait and the words *Victoria Regina Born 24th May1819 Proclaimed 20th June 1837 Crowned 28th June 1838*. Nursery-plates bearing the same inscription were also produced. The collector of Welsh ceramics should beware as very similar jugs were made in Staffordshire.

Surprisingly, the Queen's marriage to Prince Albert in 1840 was not commemorated as such. However, portrait-plates simply showing his likeness were made to the same size and pattern as the Queen's Coronation plates and may well have been produced at the time of the wedding. The portrait-plates formed part of a series which, as well as Prince Albert, also included the Revd John Wesley, the Rev John Fletcher and James Tear (or Teare – the print is found with both spellings) who was a temperance reformer.

The next commemorative to be produced was that for the royal visit to Place House at Fowey in Cornwall. From the collector's point of view, it is very interesting on a number of counts. Firstly, it was a somewhat obscure event and thus more interesting to the collector than one of national notice. Secondly, the print seems to have been used almost by default in that it is part of a series of West Country views made by the Cambrian Pottery as general souvenirs, none of the others having any commemorative connotations whatever. Thirdly, the scene, which shows the royal couple approaching Place House in an open carriage, bears the inscription *Royal Visit to Place House Fowey Sept 6th 1848*. The visit actually took place on September 8th. This rare print is found most usually on child's plates, sometimes on mugs, and very rarely on jugs.

No more commemoratives were produced in Swansea and until recently it was believed that only one true commemorative came from the South Wales Pottery at Llanelli. This was a jug to mark the death of Prince Albert in 1863. The pattern is named simply 'Albert' and the printed factory mark WTH for William Holland. The print depicts the Prince, flanked by a weeping Britannia, guarded by a very sad lion, and on the reverse side a view of Albert's greatest achievement, the Crystal Palace. These jugs are of a shape we refer to as Albert shape as they are used almost exclusively for this print. The recent discovery is a pair of plates with a shell transfer border that commemorate the marriage of the then Prince of Wales, later King Edward VII, to Princess Alexandra in 1863. Although unmarked, the shell borders and the overall characteristics of the plates make their attribution to Llanelly certain.

A small number of rather crudely printed jugs are to be found from the Llanelly factory showing a named portrait of Garibaldi. Although never marked, these jugs can be identified from the individual inscriptions applied to them (a characteristic of Llanelly Pottery at that time). Dated examples show them to have been made in the 1880s but Garibaldi's celebrated visit to Great Britain (but not in fact to Wales) took place in 1864. It seems that his popularity was undiminished and that these jugs were produced at the time of his death in 1882.

Much earlier in the factory's life the South Wales Pottery did produce very rare Wesley busts reminiscent of Staffordshire. These are discussed in more detail in the chapter on Staffordshire figures of Welsh interest.

ANTIQUARIAN MAPS
FOR THE WELSH COLLECTOR

Conrad Davies

Despite the fact that there has never been a tradition of map-making in Wales and that the number of Welsh cartographers is extremely small, anyone thinking of starting a collection of antique maps of Wales has a very wide choice. In a short article of this nature it has been necessary to be very selective. The period of map-making covered starts in 1573 when the first map of Wales to appear in an atlas was published by Abraham Ortelius and ends in 1791 when the Ordnance Survey was established. The cartographers have been selected chronologically mainly on the basis that their maps illustrate some particular development in the art and/or science of map-making. Naturally a great number of others have had to be omitted and very many interesting maps appeared after the establishment of the Ordnance Survey.

PRINTING

Initially an 'original' map would be unique as any painting or other artwork drawn by hand on paper or vellum. However, the advent of printing changed the concept of an 'original map' since multiple copies could be produced. Nowadays, an original map is one that has been made directly from the original plate.

Three basic methods have been used for the production of maps:

- Relief process – using a woodblock.

- Intaglio process – using a copper plate (later a steel plate)

- Planographic or surface printing – lithographic stone.

During the period covered by this article the normal means of production was printing on paper from a copper plate. The plate of copper used was seldom more than one-eighth of an inch thick. The image was produced on the surface of the plate by line engraving. This involved cutting a series of lines or grooves into the plate by means of a special tool called the graver. The graver was held in the palm of the hand and pushed into the copper surface to produce the lines. The pressure used on the graver would determine the depth and width of the lines and eventually light and shade in the finished print. The method was very laborious and great skill was required. In addition, the image produced on the plate had to be in reverse.

When the engraving was complete, the plate would be inked. Only the incised grooves would eventually carry ink and the surface would be wiped clean. The plate was then set in the press and printing could start. The previously dampened paper had to be pressed into the inked grooves and very great pressure was required. This caused an indentation on the outline of the metal plate resulting in the familiar platemark.

Usually the number of copies printed for each edition is not known but as many as a 1,000 or even 2,000 could be printed for one edition. Copper is a relatively soft metal and signs of wear would appear on the print after some 300 impressions. Copper plates were replaced by steel plates about 1820. This harder metal had a number of advantages – it was cheaper, facilitated finer line work and allowed at least twenty times the number of impressions before showing signs of wear.

TERMINOLOGY

An *impression* is a single example of a print taken from a plate.

Two impressions may differ because of an alteration in the plate, they are then said to be of different *states*.

An *issue* represents the total number of impressions taken at any one time from a single state of the plate.

An *edition* represents all issues printed from a particular state of a plate.

Various Latin terms and their abbreviations are traditionally used on maps to indicate the names of those concerned in their production:

cartographer, surveyor, author: *Descrip(sit); Delin(eavit); Inv(entit); Auct(ore)*

engraver: *Sc(ulpsit); Fec(it); Incid(it); Cael(avit)*. Occasionally the term *Scrip(sit)* was used for a specialist letter engraver

publisher: *Apud; Ex Officina; Ex(cudit) Formis; Sumptibus*.

COLOURING

Many publishers produced maps and atlases both coloured and uncoloured. The work of the map colourist was a respected profession. Ortelius himself was a map colourist in his early career. The majority of maps were issued uncoloured as is the case with Speed maps, although a number of special copies were coloured. In contrast, uncoloured Saxton maps are rare as nearly all were issued coloured. Maps that were issued in colour are described as 'with contemporary hand colouring', whilst maps that were coloured later are described as with 'modern colour'. Maps by Blaeu, de Witt and Jaillot with contemporary colouring, often highlighted in gold, represent the art of decorative map production at its peak.

VALUE

Antiquarian maps, like any work of art, have two values – their intrinsic value and their commercial value. The first lies in the mind of the individual. The commercial value of a map depends on a great number of factors:

- *Scarcity*: the fewer the number of copies in circulation the more expensive the map.
- *Location* greatly affects the value – a Speed map of Wales appeals to collectors from all Welsh counties, whilst that of a single county will be of particular interest to residents of that county. Likewise a map of Glamorganshire will be more expensive than a similar one of Radnorshire.
- In general the *older* the map the greater its value – the earlier editions of a particular map are usually more expensive. There are exceptions where a late edition might have been very limited and therefore fewer copies are available.
- Other important factors are the *condition* of the map and the quality of the colouring, if coloured.

A complete Speed Atlas could be bought in 1920 for £3.50. One was auctioned in London in November 1995 for £33,000.

THE MAPS AND THE MAP-MAKERS

Humphrey Llwyd, 1527-1568

The first individual map of Wales to be published appeared in 1573. It was contained in a supplement to Abraham Ortelius' world atlas 'Theatrum Orbis Terrarum'. The map was based on manuscripts sent to Ortelius by Humphrey Llwyd of Denbigh.

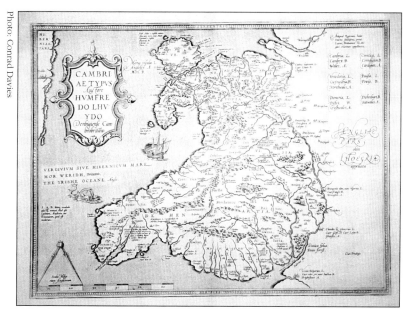

Humphrey Llwyd's map of Wales, printed 1584.

It would appear that in the first instance Llwyd was asked by Ortelius for some notes on the island of Mona (Anglesey). Before he completed the work he intended to send to Ortelius, he was taken ill in the summer of 1568 and wrote providing details of Anglesey and also an illustrated description of Wales together with a map of England. This material was sent to Ortelius before Llwyd died in August 1568 at the age of 41.

Llwyd's map as it appeared in 1573 was the first printed showing the coast of Wales in anything like its true form. Nevertheless, there are a number of gross errors. No doubt many of these would have been corrected had Llwyd survived to the time of publication. To mention but a few anomalies, the Lleyn Peninsula is peculiarly distorted; St Bride's Bay and the Gower Peninsula are almost completely suppressed. The border between England and Wales is such that much of the Marches is included in Wales so that South Wales appears much larger than North Wales. The names of the rivers Rheidol and Ystwyth are transposed. Some towns, such as Merthyr Tydfil and Caerphilly, are wrongly located.

The three principal regions of Wales are delineated – Venedotia (Gwynedd), Povisia (Powys) and Dehenbartia (Deheubarth). The thirteen Welsh counties do not appear although they were established as administrative units by this time. An interesting feature of Llwyd's map is that three languages are used – Latin, Welsh and English. This is in keeping with Llwyd's view that a map should illustrate the history as well as the geography of Wales. Many towns are given two or three names, for example, Menevia; Saynt Davyes; Ty Dhewy for St David's. A number of notes of historical interest also appear on the map. No roads are shown.

Despite its many deficiencies Humphrey Llwyd's map of Wales was very popular and was reprinted nearly 50 times between 1573 and 1741.

Christopher Saxton, 1542-1610

The first printed county maps of Wales were published by Christopher Saxton in his 'Atlas of England and Wales' in 1579.

Born in Yorkshire about 1542, educated at Cambridge, Saxton was a land surveyor by profession. He eventually moved to London. In 1570 he was commissioned to produce a complete survey of England and Wales under the patronage of Sir Thomas Seckford and with the approval of Queen Elizabeth.

In 1576 when he was ready to survey Wales he was provided with an Open Letter addressed to '*all Justices of the Peace, Mayors and Others*' asking that they '*shall be aiding and assisting unto him to see him conducted unto any Towre, Castle, highe place or hill to view that countrey and that he may be accompanied by honest men such as do best know the countrey*'. A request was also made to provide a Welsh and English-speaking horseman to conduct Saxton to the next town. Undoubtedly, one of the major difficulties he encountered was that of language, and the place-names would have been noted 'by ear'. The importance of Saxton's Atlas cannot be overemphasised and the majority of maps produced for

Photo: Carmarthenshire County Museum, Abergwili, Carmarthen

Llanelly Pottery: variations on cockerel plates. Left: the traditional cockerel of Sarah Roberts; right: the work of Samuel Shufflebotham.

Photo: Robert Pugh Antiques/John Fry

Swansea Pottery (Cambrian). Left: an example of 'Glamorgan' with rare natural colouring; right: a typical example of Cambrian work with splashes of pink lustre.

Dillwyn's Etruscan Ware: an amphora made of clay from Penllergaer, Swansea. Size: 14½" (37cm).

Commemorative pottery, Swansea Pottery (Cambrian): a child's mug commemorating Queen Victoria's Coronation; a child's plate showing Prince Albert (perhaps on the occasion of his marriage); Llanelly Pottery: a pink transfer jug commemorating Garibaldi.

the next hundred years were based on Saxton's survey. Saxton's maps were published in various issues up to 1770.

Only three Welsh counties were published separately – Monmouthshire, Glamorganshire and Pembrokeshire. Interesting features of the maps include the fine engraving with two lettering styles – capitals for larger towns and cities, lower case for the remainder. The sea appears stippled. Hills are depicted as sugarloaves, parks are bounded by fencing. Neither administrative boundaries nor roads are shown.

William Kip and William Hole

Saxton's maps were used in a reduced form to illustrate the sixth edition of William Camden's 'Britannia' in 1607. For the first time the thirteen Welsh counties are represented on separate sheets. The maps were engraved by two English engravers, William Kip and William Hole, and nearly all the maps were based on Saxton's survey. Pembrokeshire is an exception; this was based on the description of George Owen of Henllys.

Maps from the 1607 edition are printed on a thin paper and the text on the reverse side may show through. The first English edition was published in 1610, the maps with blank backs and with plate numbers added to most maps. In the 1637 edition the map of Breconshire was from a new plate engraved by Robert Vaughan. These maps again had blank backs.

These first maps of the Welsh counties emphasise the invaluable contribution made by Saxton. They predate Speed's maps and from a commercial point of view are greatly undervalued.

John Speed, 1552-1629

The most popular and best known of all the Welsh county maps are undoubtedly those of John Speed. All these maps are based on Saxton's survey and Speed readily acknowledged that he had *'put my sickle in other men's corne . . .'*

Speed, however, incorporated town plans based on first hand information gained '. . . *by my own travels through every province in England and Wales mine eyes have beheld*'. In addition, the boundaries of the hundreds are delineated on all but three county maps (Denbigh, Fflint and Caernarfonshire, where he was denied access to the Sheriff's records). A descriptive text appears on the back of each based largely on Camden's Britannia.

Speed had no patron and the commercial success of the venture depended on the number of atlases and maps he could sell. He entrusted the great Dutch engraver Jodocus Hondius with the work. He provided Hondius with a rich and varied miscellany of illustrations – town plans, portraits, costume designs, heraldry, battle scenes.

The great success and decorative excellence of Speed's maps is largely due to the great skill of Hondius and his craftsmen. Another development was the use of a border to incorporate matter not forming part of the map, as seen on the map of Wales. Speed's atlas was first published in 1612 under the title 'The Theatre of the Empire of Great Britain'. A number of county maps show the date 1611 and appeared with this date in much later editions of the Atlas. It was comprised of four books, the second of which covered Wales. The title page reads: '*The Second Booke containing The Pricipalitie of Wales, delivering An exact Topographie of the Covnties Divisions of their Cantreves and Commots Descriptions of their Cities and Shire-Townes with A Compendious Relation of things most memorable in every of them. Performed by John Speed*'. The maps were published as late as 1770 covering a period of 158 years. Roads were incorporated in the later editions.

Pieter van den Keere, c.1571-1646

In 1599 the Dutch cartographer Pieter van den Keere prepared a set of miniature maps based on Saxton's survey. At the time the venture came to nothing. The plates were later acquired by George Humble who published Speed's maps. He eventually published van den Keere's maps and described them as 'from a Larger Volume done by John Speede'; a clear example of early 17th century entrepreneurship since van den Keere's plates pre-dated Speed's. Humble was astute enough a businessman to take advantage of the popularity of Speed's atlas to help sales of the 'miniature Speeds' as they are called.

THE DUTCH SCHOOL

Joan Blaeu, 1596-1673 and and Jan Jansson, 1588-1664

The most famous name among the Dutch map publishers is that of Blaeu. Starting from the small establishment of Wilhelm Blaeu the business expanded under the two sons Joan and Cornelius to become one of the most prolific map publishing houses ever seen. The premises contained hand type-presses, a type foundry, plate storage rooms, paper making rooms, rooms for plate and book-binding, rooms for proof reading, washing type and drying sheets, binding in vellum covers and so on.

The firm of Hondius and associates was in competition with Blaeu and Jan Jansson, Hondius' son-in-law, became involved in the rivalry. Despite, or because of, the fierce competition, no original cartography emerged. Old plates or plates copied from earlier maps were freely used and publishers were constantly under pressure to be first to produce a particular regional atlas.

In 1635 Blaeu's atlas was published in two volumes with editions in four languages. For the next 30 years Blaeu and Jansson ran a parallel course vying with each other. Eventually, each produced World Atlases in 11-12 volumes. Their fourth volume contained maps of the British Isles mainly copied from Speed.

Blaeu's map of Wales shows the coats of arms of the four Welsh dioceses of that time. Not all the Welsh counties are printed on separate sheets.

In terms of skills in engraving and calligraphy, composition and balance of the finished product the maps of Bleau have never been equalled and are regarded as the pinnacle of decorative map production. Undoubtedly, the primacy of the Dutch cartographers and map-publishers of the 17th century was fully justified. The de Witts, Schenk and Valk, Visschers and Ottens were other important Dutch map makers of the century.

John Ogilby, 1600-1675

John Ogilby may be regarded as the most important British carto-grapher since Saxton. He published the first atlas of road maps of any country.

Born in Edinburgh, he had been dance master, private tutor, theatre owner and publisher before starting on his work on the road maps at the age of 65. Ogilby was concerned with the Post Roads used for conveying letters to and from London. His 'Britannia' con-tained 100 strip road maps showing in great detail rivers, bridges, ferries, hills, county boundaries, unfenced roads, moors, bogs, etc.

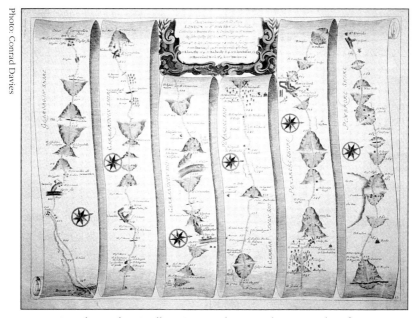

Road map by Ogilby; Carmarthen to Aberystwyth, 1675.

He was the first cartographer to employ the statute mile of 1,760 yards, the scale of the map being one inch to a mile. To help the user to interpret the maps Ogilby explained '*We have projected them (roads) upon imaginary scrolls, the initial City or Town being always at the bottom of the outermost scroll on the left-hand; whence your road ascends again, thus constantly ascending till it terminates at the top of the outermost scroll on the right hand*'.

Britannia was first published in 1675 (three editions) with another edition in 1698. 14 of the hundred road maps enter or traverse a Welsh county. Ogilby's maps were copied by many later cartographers and produced in a reduced form convenient for travellers.

Robert Morden, flourished 1695-1703

The new edition of Camden's Britannia published in 1695 was illustrated by Robert Morden. This was possibly the first atlas from a new survey since Saxton's maps. There were no county maps of Wales other than Monmouthshire. Wales was illustrated by a map of North Wales and another of South Wales.

Morden's maps are of significance because they were the first to use London (St Paul's) as the prime meridian. He also indicated a system of roads. Three scales of miles are shown – great, middle and small.

Thomas Kitchin, 1718-1784

The partnership of Emmanuel Bowen and Thomas Kitchin represents the most significant co-operative British cartographic venture of the 18th century. Both were skilled engravers and both produced many maps and atlases of their own.

Their Large English Atlas published in 1753 contained maps of six South Wales counties only but represent the finest and most detailed county maps of the 18th century. It would seem that Kitchin made a great effort to obtain patronage to ensure the commercial success of the venture. To this end he not only noted houses and farms but also the names of the people that lived there.

Hills were represented by hachuring – the closer the lines, the steeper the slopes. Roads were marked with distances and a great wealth of notes of interest were included on the map. Many include a panoramic view of a city or town reduced from the views of Samuel and Nathaniel Buck.

John Owen & Emmanuel Bowen, flourished 1750

Emmanuel Bowen was one of the most prolific and skilled engravers of the 18th century. One of his earliest work was published in 1720 as 'Britannia Depicta'. This contained a county map of each of the counties of England and Wales and over 200 road maps.

The maps were published by John Owen. Unfortunately, rarely do the road maps on the back relate to the county map on the front, Pembrokeshire being an exception. Below the county map details of the county appear – size, climate, industry, etc.

John Cary, 1754-1834

In 1759 the newly formed Society of Arts offered an annual prize for an accurate survey of any English county on a scale of 1 inch to 1 mile. This gave an incentive for the production of large scale maps. It also heralded a period of tremendous activity in new and accurate surveying.

John Cary was one of the most skilful cartographers of this era running up to the establishment of the Ordnance Survey. His maps have a clarity and delicacy of line with absence of irrelevant material which gives them a 'modern' look although they were produced over 200 years ago. There are maps of South Wales and North Wales but no county maps.

William Owen (Pughe), 1759-1835

In 1788 William Owen, born in Meirionethshire, produced two maps of Wales engraved by Thomas Conder to Illustrate Mr Warrington's 'The History of Wales'. These maps were 'A map of Wales according to the Ancient Divisions of Gwynedd, Powis and Dinefwr with their respective Cantrevs subdivided into Comots' and 'A Map of Wales according to the Modern Divisions of Counties'.

The former map gives details of the major and minor administrative divisions which might have been taken from a list reputedly edited by Humphrey Llwyd. The second map illustrates the twelve Welsh counties delineated after the Act of Union of 1536. Monmouthshire is not included, reflecting the ambiguity regarding the status of this county. A feature of both the maps is that the orthography of Welsh place-names is a very great improvement on that found in all earlier maps of Wales.

Ordnance Survey

The Ordnance Survey was officially established in 1791 and was first known as the Trigonometrical Survey. In its early days it had two tasks. The first was to carry out the Great Triangulation, which was achieved between 1798 and 1853. Two base lines were established, one on the shores of Lough Foyle (1827) and the other on Salisbury Plain (1849). When a test base was measured at Lossiemouth in 1909 it was found that the error on any side of this triangulation did not exceed 1" in a mile. The second requirement was the production of the one inch to the mile maps.

The first few sheets were issued in 1801 covering Kent, part of Essex and London. The purpose of the map was largely military. It was not until 1870 that it covered the whole of Britain. Carmarthenshire was printed in 1831.

The work of the Ordnance Survey is a massive study in its own right and marked a new beginning to the whole work of mapmaking.

Lewis Morris, 1701-1765
William Morris, 1737-1779

'*Y rhai ant mewn Llongau i'r Donn a'u taith uwch Mawrion Ddyfroedd a Welsant ryfeddodau'r Ior, a hyn mewn Eigion Moroedd'.* Psalm 107, v. 23 and 24. These verses appear on the title page of 'Plans of Harbours, Bars, Bays and Roads in St George's Channel' by Lewis Morris, published in 1748.

The plate showing 'The North Entrance of Bardsey Sound and the Roads' carries a verse in the lower right hand comer of the page:

> *Os anodd ar Gaswenan*
> *droi ar Lif o'r Dŵr i'r Lan*
> *Anaws na myned yno*
> *troi Bun o'r natur y bo. R Leia 1450*

Perhaps these verses more than anything demonstrate the Welshness of Lewis Morris (Llewellyn Ddu o Fôn), one of the famous and talented brothers from Anglesey (Morysiaid Môn).

The charts were the result of a survey carried out by Lewis Morris under directions of the Lords of the Admiralty. This hydrographic atlas is worthy of note since it represents the work of one of the very few Welsh cartographers. In his introduction Morris says 'The melancholy accounts of shipwrecks and Losses so frequent on the coast of Wales made it necessary for the Admiralty to take the same into consideration and determine that an actual survey of that coast should be made. And in 1737 they were pleased to order me upon that service'. Lewis Morris' survey covered the coast between Llandudno and Milford Haven.

The book published in 1748 contained 24 charts together with detailed trade statistics, suggestions for the improvement of ports and a Welsh alphabet for the use of English traders.

In 1801 William Morris published a revised edition of his father's work extending the survey as far as Liverpool in the north and

Photo: Conrad Davies

Frontispiece of Lewis Morris's Atlas, 1748.

Swansea and Neath in the south. A plan of the Bay and Harbour of Dublin was also included.

CONCLUSION

The maps described above represent a very small fraction of the maps available to the Welsh collector. They illustrate some of the important changes during the period from Ortelius to Ordnance Survey.

Humphrey Llwyd's was the first map of Wales but was not based on a survey. Christopher Saxton made the first comprehensive survey of Wales and most maps for the next hundred years were based on his survey. The maps of Kip and Hole based on Saxton's survey provided the first maps of all individual Welsh counties. John Speed incorporated town plans as part of his county maps and a wealth of decorative material. The Dutch school represented by Blaeu and Jansson illustrated the ultimate in the art of decorative map-making but no cartographic progress.

John Ogilby broke new ground with the introduction of his strip
road maps based on actual surveys. An important feature was the
use of the statute mile. Robert Morden again used new survey data
and used London as the prime meridian. Roads were marked.
Kitchin and Bowen also used new survey material, hachuring to
represent relief, marked roads with distances and included a wealth
of information on their maps. (Mercator would regard the latter as a
retrograde step in map-making). The maps of William Owen Pughe
provide maps of Wales where due regard is given to the correct
spelling of Welsh place-names. The sea charts of Lewis and William
Morris represent examples of the work of hydrographers and one of
particular interest because the authors were Welsh.

Anyone starting a collection is well advised to decide on a particular theme or interest in order to limit the scope of the collection.
Some examples would be maps of a limited geographic area, perhaps a county or group of counties; maps by a particular cartographer;
road maps; railway maps; canal maps; sea charts or maps produced
during a particular period of time. The choice must be an individual
one. The collecting of maps must give pleasure and a growing
interest which may develop into a passion. Surely, no one can fail
to get that 'tingle factor' from studying and handling a map produced in one of the great map-houses 300 to 400 years ago.

WELSH SAMPLERS

Ann Dorsett

MANY WELSH HOMES still display with pride a family sampler or two. Mostly, these samplers date from the nineteenth century and were made at school by very young girls. Early nineteenth century samplers can be very attractive and very fine. Learning how to sew neatly was a vital part of the education of the Victorian schoolgirl. In the days before sewing machines or mass-produced garments, who else could make household linen and underwear but the housewife and her daughters? Those girls who went into service as maids were also expected to do their share of mending or sewing for the larger house or farm. The invention of the sewing machine, printed and fancy woven fabrics, and mass production prompted a marked decline in the quality of samplers. As learning how to sew became less essential, sampler makers began to combine crude stitchery with rough fabrics, thick woollen thread and poor design.

Sampler making also played a vital role in teaching sewing before the Victorian era. Women learnt through sampler making how to use different stitches for garment making, for marking linen or embroidery. The earliest samplers were collections of embroidered patterns, motifs and stitches arranged at random on a piece of linen. The word 'sampler', which was in use by the 16th century, derives from the Latin 'exemplar', denoting its use as something to work from. The earliest, surviving (and exceptionally rare) Welsh embroideries date from the sixteenth and seventeenth centuries, although no samplers survive from the period. Although none survive, it is known that earlier Welsh princes and noblemen shared a fashionable love of lavishly embroidered clothes and hangings with the rest of mediaeval nobility. Welsh poems and literature of the time abound with references to these treasured embroideries. The fifteenth century poet, Lewis Glyn Cothi describes in a poem, '. . a cloth full of designs – saplings, leaves, birds of the earth, lions. Below are stags and cross designs . . . green clover leaves, French gardens . . . a leopard and moons . . .'. Fancy embroidery was also imported from abroad, bringing new designs, and exotic ones at that, into the country. By the seventeenth century, Welsh embroiderers were embroidering tent curtains and bed linen, as well as three-dimensional stump work. Designs for these embroideries and their component stitches would have been recorded on samplers.

Designs for the motifs in embroideries and sampler records came from a number of sources. Originality is sometimes seen in these embroideries but this is the exception. Indeed, samplers often contain designs with very ancient antecedents in heraldry or illuminated manuscripts. Early patterns for embroidery came from mediaeval manuscripts but later, printed book illustrations were copied. The earliest pattern book had been a translation of 1591 of an Italian work, illustrating that patterns for sampler making are not regional, but are international in origin. In the seventeenth century, in England and Wales, Shorleyker's *Scholehouse for the Needle*, 1624 and James Boler's *The Needle's Excellency*, 1640 were the most popular printed, pattern books. The earliest samplers made using these pattern books were long and narrow, sometimes over a yard long. Not designed for display, these samplers were kept rolled up on ivory rods, ready to be taken out when needed. They contained geometrical and floral patterns, worked in coloured silks or metallic threads. Fillings of needlepoint lace, drawn work and white-work were often incorporated into the samplers. Long inscriptions are not found on seventeenth century samplers but the maker often included her own name and the date. The letters of the alphabet also became part of the sampler maker's repertoire at this time.

Samplers of the seventeenth century were made by adults in the home, but by the end of the eighteenth century sampler making had become almost exclusively restricted to schoolchildren. This is evident in those eighteenth century English and Welsh samplers that have survived showing the maker's name, her age and the date. A gradual change also took place during the eighteenth century in the appearance of the sampler, as it changed from a reference vehicle into an item for display. Samplers became shorter and squarer, and ornamental borders were introduced. Interestingly, although made in schools, few eighteenth or nineteenth century samplers have obvious educational value, except for samplers embroidered in the form of maps of England and Wales and Biblical verses. In general, samplers became the schoolgirl's diploma and could be hung on the wall, as a permanent, framed example of her skill as a house-wife. Lessons in needlework began at an early age in school. 'Baby threaders', or special short needles with blunt tips were given to children of as young as five. While most school sewing would have been everyday work, it is the fancy, presentation pieces, the framed samplers, which have survived in large numbers.

Framed samplers, particularly those of 1800 until 1870 are fasci-nating. Each has a story to tell and they are surprisingly varied and often very finely sewn. At the end of the eighteenth century a cream-coloured, woollen, tammy cloth became popular as a ground for embroidery, replacing the drabber linen and brightening the appear-ance of the sampler. Samplers of this period were sewn in coloured silks, using cross stitch, eyelet stitch and satin stitch. Motifs of the eighteenth century sampler were retained into the nineteenth century. A certain uniformity of design began to be seen in the nineteenth century, as makers adopted a design formula of a large central motif surrounded by other, smaller, scattered motifs. Pictorial designs, such as figures of Adam and Eve in the Garden of Eden and pictures of houses also became popular. One of Carmarthenshire County Museum's finest samplers was completed by Mary Lewis 'in the 13/ year of her age/July 1834'. Mary Lewis was a pupil at Miss Hughes's school at the time and this may be the large red, Georgian house in

A 19th century sampler with a large central motif of the *Princess Royal* surrounded by smaller scattered motifs.

the centre of the sampler (although it seems unlikely that a dame's school would have been in such an impressive building). Mary Lewis also embroidered figures of Adam and Eve standing under the Tree of Knowledge. Like the birds and potted plants, they are old patterns used again and again in samplers and embroideries over the centuries.

Equally impressive is the sampler by Margaret Davies of Cwrt y Cadno (collection Carmarthenshire County Museum), which she completed when she was nineteen years old in 1853. This big sampler is dominated by a large sailing ship, named by Margaret Davies as the 'Brins Royal' but probably the 'Princess Royal'. Beneath the ship is a

Georgian house flanked by the figures of a man and woman in eighteenth century dress. These seem to be Adam and Eve, as they are marked with the initials 'A' and an 'E'. Margaret Davies's sampler is full of spelling errors, which seems strange when one considers the hours of painstaking work put into the sampler. The most likely explanation is that the embroideress was not working in her first language of Welsh, and indeed some of the spelling is distinctly Welsh. Welsh language samplers from this date are rare, as it seems that Welsh schools applied the 'Welsh Not' rule to sewing as well the rest of school life. Those samplers that have verses in Welsh upon them are fairly recent or were sewn at home. Miserable or morbid verses were common in schoolgirl samplers, and Margaret Davies's is no exception. She has copied out a Biblical verse from Ecclesiastes 12 which was often used by sampler makers. Margaret Davies's version of the verse is incomplete. It should read 'Remember now thy Creator in the days of thy youth, while the evil days come not, nor the years draw nigh'. What a thoroughly depressing verse for a young child to copy.

One of the prettiest samplers in Carmarthenshire County Museum's collection is a very finely embroidered sampler sewn in tiny cross stitches on cream wool. Remarkably, the sampler was made by a little girl of ten, Sarah Ann Doidge, and she has embroidered the following touching dedication to her teacher: 'Under the instruction of a sincere and affectionate friend M. A. Ryder'. We can only guess at the age of this sampler, although it was probably made during the 1840s, as the date is missing. At the age of sixty-five, Sarah Ann Doidge exercised her privilege and unpicked the date, to conceal her age from her friends.

The nineteenth century also saw changes in the stitches employed in sampler making. In the early 1800s they continued to be embroidered in a variety of stitches but by 1850, most were sewn entirely in cross stitch. So universal was the use of cross stitch that it was popularly known as 'sampler' stitch. Unbleached canvas had already taken the place of the woollen ground. Most later nineteenth century

A colourful cross stitch sampler.
Made in Carmarthen in 1860 by Mary Jones.

Collection/Photo: Carmarthenshire County Museum, Abergwili, Carmarthen

cross stitch samplers are embroidered in wool and on a coarse-meshed canvas. In technique, these samplers resemble the popular Berlin woolwork pictures (the name derives from the brightly coloured wools that were imported from Berlin for the making of these needleworks). Victorian embroideresses lavished hours of their time slavishly copying reproductions of famous paintings or popular prints from squared paper to produce highly naturalistic, embroidered pictures. Some of this naturalistic representation soon found its way into sampler making. However, this mechanical copying and simple stitchery led to a decline in the standard of stitchery and design in samplers. By 1900, the age of the sampler was over. Sampler making survives today as a skilled and pleasant pastime, a far cry from its original purpose. Nothing illustrates better the enormous changes that have taken place in the education of women than the history of the sampler.

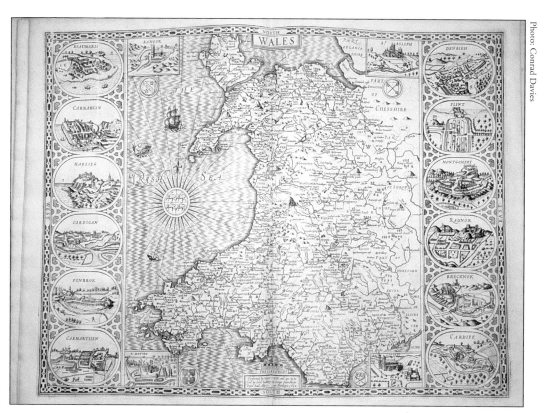

A map of Wales by John Speed; printed in 1676.

A sampler from Cydweli (Kidwelly).

Welsh Porcelain (from left): a Swansea plate probably decorated by Henry Morris; a Swansea porcelain plate with Regency design decorated in London; a Swansea porcelain plate with Mandarin design; the edge shows the crest of the Lloyd family.

A carved treen spoon and fork set, with balls in cages; from the second half of the nineteenth century. An unusually small love spoon, carved from sheep's bone; dated 1849, from Llanboidy.

Photo: John Fry

FIGURES
ON A MANTELPIECE
Victorian Staffordshire Figures in a Welsh Context

Carol Pugh

S TAFFORDSHIRE FIGURES were probably one of the most familiar sights on the mantlepiece of any Victorian home. These brightly coloured ornaments, made in their thousands at hundreds of unidentified potteries in Staffordshire, have an understated, naive charm which has endured throughout the last hundred and fifty years. They provide a popular and rewarding field for collectors today.

Those who care to look beneath the unsophisticated exterior of Staffordshire figures will find a potted pictorial history of social, political and domestic life during the 19th century. While many were purely ornamental, some were inscribed with names, and huge numbers of what are described as 'portrait figures' have now been identified as being associated with famous (and infamous) people, places and events in history.

Today's collector, with such a wide range of subjects to choose from, inevitably decides to collect figures with a common theme. Thus, collections are put together of naval or royal figures, theatrical figures or politicians, religious reformers or criminals. There are, however, interesting pieces to be found from a number of these categories which relate directly to Wales, and reflect some of its own history and culture during the second half of the 19th century.

The Victorian Staffordshire figures as we know them were, in fact, produced from the 1830s. At this time they were a mass-produced, rather gaudy development of the earlier, more finely potted and sympathetically coloured pottery figures of the late 18th and early 19th centuries. Technical developments, such as the ability to produce the characteristic, bright under-glazed cobalt blue colour which gave these figures mass-appeal, meant that they could be produced cheaply and in quantity by relatively unskilled workers. As the century progressed, so the techniques were streamlined until each one required just two moulds and the only detailed moulding and decoration was applied to the front of the figure. Hence the familiar term 'flatbacks', by which they are often referred today. Hardly ever found with a factory mark, their importance was, no doubt, only ever intended to be transient.

Their subject matter came from a wide diversity of sources. It was a time of great progress in the printing industry and publishers of prints, either for the home or, more commercially, for advertising plays, circuses and other travelling entertainments, provided the source matter for many figures, along with illustrated papers and music covers.

Few people could read, and less had access to newspapers or periodicals and so newsworthy stories of the time were conveyed by word of mouth. Enterprising pottery owners would be on the look-out for something to catch the imagination of their potters, and thus Royal marriages, gruesome murders and melodramatic stories involving heroes, children or animals (preferably all three) quickly manifested themselves in clay. The results were usually lively figures with unrestrained decoration, often bearing mis-spelled titles. Figures were distributed though travelling fairs, markets and shops, while street vendors would probably have taken up strategic positions outside theatres and circuses to hawk their wares.

South Wales had its own flourishing pottery industry at this time but curiously did not get involved in the production of figures (with one notable exception). We know that pottery workers travelled to Wales from the traditional centres around Stoke, so no doubt the skill was available. We also know that there was a considerable market for Staffordshire figures in Wales. The number of figures still to be found in the Principality bears this out. Their bright, cheerful appeal is similar to that of lustre pottery and it was particularly at home on oak furniture in candle-lit cottages. It is not surprising, therefore, that a number of figures were obviously made principally for the Welsh market, and they make an interesting collection.

Inevitably, portrait figures of Welsh interest are largely of a religious nature. This may not have been entirely coincidental – the spirit of John Wesley was alive and well and living with the poor of Staffordshire, their place of manufacture. Indeed, Anthony Oliver (whose two excellent books are probably responsible for much of the current interest in Staffordshire figures) described it as 'a country of pubs, primitive Methodism and premature death'. These travelling clerical figures carried a stern message and their influence resulted in a demand for figures which the Staffordshire potters were only too happy to supply. They are scarce now and they each deserve their place here.

John Bryan was born at Llanfyllin in 1770 and became a Methodist at about the turn of the 18th century. He preached in England and Wales for thirteen years before setting up as a grocer in Yorkshire, and subsequently in Caernarvon. Here he preached, brilliantly we are told, until his death in 1856.

The figure of John Bryan shows an uninspiring, short, stout, balding man dressed entirely in black, his right hand holds a bible, and is resting on a brick pillar. His name is moulded on the base.

The decoration of these religious figures are similar in decoration. The black frock-coats and breeches are coloured with a pigment applied *over* the glaze. This black was, therefore, vulnerable to flaking and this sort of damage can be disfiguring. Most other colours were applied under the glaze which protects them from damage. Condition is an important consideration when contemplating a purchase.

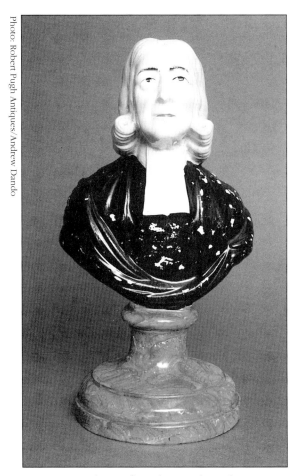

Photo: Robert Pugh Antiques/Andrew Dando

Rare bust of Wesley made at the
South Wales Pottery, Llanelly.

Christmas Evans was the famous, charismatic preacher who begar
his working life as a farm labourer. His distinctive appearance owed
much to the loss of an eye in a religious brawl when he was 22. Fo
many years a Baptist minister in Anglesey, he had a reputation as
strict disciplinarian and it was said that when he preached hellfire
you could feel the heat! He died in 1838.

A large (13½"), imposing figure, Christmas Evans wears a black
frock-coat and, in the manner of many other clerical and academi
figures, rests one arm on books on a pillar. His right eye is close
and his hair curls over his forehead, bearing a remarkable resem
blance to a contemporary line-engraved portrait.

John Elias, an itinerant preacher, taught in the first Sunday school in Caernarvonshire and published religious tracts. A Calvinistic Methodist, in 1823 he participated in drawing up the Methodists' articles of faith.

The figure of John Elias is probably the pair to Christmas Evans, and probably originates from the same source. He adopts a similar stance alongside a stone pillar, holding a bible in his left hand. Both this and the Christmas Evans figure have matching rectangular bases bearing their names in raised capital letters. It is a tribute to these preachers' enduring reputation that these figures were probably produced in the 1850s, some 15 or so years after their deaths.

Christmas Evans.

Photo: National Museums and Galleries of Wales

Robert Trogwy Evans enjoyed a considerable reputation and was a powerful force in the Temperance movement. A Congregationalist, he ministered in Manchester during the 1850s, then in Greenfield, Flintshire until 1870, after which he emigrated to the United States.

His figure shows a distinguished gentleman once again in rather classical pose beside a pillar. Beneath his black jacket he sports a floral waistcoat, the overall effect being decidedly non-clerical.

It is an interesting indiosyncracy of Staffordshire portrait figures that occasionally a model will be re-used in another guise, presumably in the interests of speed and economy! An almost identical figure to Robert Trogwy Evans, similarly decorated, was produced at about the same time (c.1856) bearing the name of William Palmer, the famous Rugeley poisoner! The two men were of approximately the same age and in an effort to capitalise on the furore surrounding conviction of Palmer for the murders of his wife, brother and friend, it was possible that a pottery decided to use the same model as Robert Evans in the safe hope that they were unlikely to be bought by the same customers!

They did not account for their descendants, over a hundred years later, exposing their subterfuge with a certain wry admiration for their opportunism!

Evan Roberts was born near Loughor, close to Llanelly in 1878 the son of a miner. After training for the ministry at Newcastle Emlyn, and undergoing psychic experiences, he launched a revivalist movement at Loughor. He went on to become a controversial member of the religious revival movement which engulfed Wales during the early years of this century.

His figure was probably produced in about 1905 at the height of this revival. It is crude and simplistic in the nature of these late Staffordshire figures, but retains the characteristics of the other clerics with his black frock coat and supporting plinth. Despite its simplicity, it also shows a remarkable resemblance to a photograph of the young man published at about this time. Unlike many post Victorian figures, which became coarse in design and decoration, this figure of Evan Roberts maintains the style of earlier examples. His name is written in elaborate, copper-plate script on the base.

None of these preachers would have a place in history had it not been for the father of Methodism, John Wesley himself. Although not of Welsh origin, his style of evangelism found a ready audience in the oppressed industrial workers of the late 18th century and, as such, he deserves a place in any collection of figures relating to Wales and its heritage. Miners, ironworkers, spinners, weavers and potters all converted in huge numbers to his simple doctrine. It was, therefore, inevitable that he was glorified by the potters of Stafford-shire in a variety of figures throughout most of the 19th century. Often depicted in a rather elaborate pulpit, one hand raised in admonition, he is usually flanked by angels, and sometimes incon-gruously surmounts a painted clock-face.

During the closing years of the 18th century, towards the end of his life, some fine quality busts of Wesley were produced. These were realistically modelled and coloured and, indeed, similar versions of these were made well into the 19th century, although with dimin-ishing quality. And it is here that a strange, and rather exciting, anomaly occurs.

For in the very early days of the South Wales Pottery at Llanelly a bust of Wesley was produced by that factory. It was of the fine quality associated with the products of Staffordshire at the end of the previous century, clearly marked (SOUTH WALES POTTERY) and mounted on a classical base, or socle, painted to resemble red-grained marble. Nothing of this nature had been produced before or since by any of the South Wales factories, and only two such busts have, to date, come to light. It is remarkable in that its very production required moulds and techniques not normally used in the production of the factory's other wares at that time. Perhaps some potter newly arrived from Staffordshire wanted to impress with his skills, or perhaps it was made in commemoration of some long-forgotten local celebration.

The Staffordshire potters also produced a vast range of little model houses and castles. Often adorned with climbing plants, they were invariably hopelessly romanticised and out of proportion. Sometimes they too were part of a story in the news. Houses which had witnessed gruesome murders were given an appropriate title, as were some castles. These may well have been the fore-runners of holiday souvenirs bought by those taking advantage of the spread-ing network of the new railway system. Two such deserve a place in our collection.

Caernarvon Castle is probably as splendid now as it was when it was built in the late 13th century. Some of its dignity was undoubtedly captured by the Staffordshire potters in its imposing towers and many windows. Made in the 1850s, its importance is denoted by the plaque on its base bearing its name in raised capital letters.

Beaumaris Castle was also recreated fairly faithfully showing its gate next to the sea. This also bears a plaque with its name.

Our final category of figures must come under the general heading of 'Romantic'. Characters from Welsh folklore such as Ned Morgan, Jenny Jones and faithful Gelert have all been immortalised in clay, along with numerous Welsh farmers, their wives, Shepherds and Hunters.

The familiar story of Edward Morgan the ploughman and his sweetheart Jenny Jones captured the imagination of architect Charles James Matthews when, in 1825 he went to live at Pontblyddyn Farm, Llangollen where he found the loving couple. The touching tale of Ned's return after twenty years in the Navy to marry his childhood sweetheart was translated into a ballad by Matthews. He set it to the tune of *Cader Idris* and, several years later it was performed, to great acclaim on the London stage by Matthews who had, by then, turned his talents to acting.

The Ballad of Edward Morgan and Jenny Jones caught the public's attention and was popular for some twenty years. During this time the Staffordshire potters interpreted this interest into a variety of figures depicting the couple. One such pair are named in gilt script and show Jenny Jones carrying a milk pail and wearing the tradition tall hat and shawl. Ned Morgan, on the other hand, is in typical Victorian sailor's garb. He stands beside a three-legged table bearing an ale jug and raises a large tankard in his right hand. Another, most attractive coloured group shows Ned and Jenny either side of a rather large milestone bearing the inscription 'LANGOLEN 1 MILE' (*sic*).

An interesting insight into the wealth of detail which potters were prepared to incorporate into these simple ornaments is borne out by research (carried out by Anthony Oliver) regarding a curious group depicting who we now know to be Ned Morgan and Jenny Jones. Ned stands convivially with one leg on a chair and tankard in hand. His left hand is round the shoulder of Jenny Jones, who is sits behind a small table, covered with a cloth. On the table is a round cheese and she is cutting a loaf of bread! The words of the ballad written by Matthews mentions the happy couple living '. . . *on our cheese and our ale in contentment* . . .'. This cheerful figure makes them appear content indeed!

It is a tribute to the potter or model-maker, who probably knew the words of this ballad by heart, that they were able to condense so much detail into such a simple ornament!

The heart-rending story of Gelert was exactly the stuff which inspired the Staffordshire potters to produce some of their most charming pieces.

The story originates in the 13th century when King John presented Prince Llewelyn with a hound called Gelert. This faithful companion was mistakenly blamed for the death of the Prince's son, who had just wandered off. But poor Gelert, blood-spattered after a fight with a wolf, was slain before the Prince realised his mistake. The child re- turned safely and in his remorse Prince Llewelyn buried Gelert in great style and called his resting- place Beddgelert.

Jenny Jones and Ned Morgan.

The origins of this story are not clear, but it was apparently resur- rected in the 19th century when the taste for such melodrama resulted in such stories being published and illustrated with fine engravings. It was to these that many potters looked for inspiration and one such figure of Gelert shows a well modelled hound sitting protectively alongside a child, the body of a wolf lying at his feet. Another version exemplifies the ever-practical Victorian Staffordshire potter in full flight of fancy. A watch-holder is behind this glorious arrangement of brightly-coloured, tassled curtains and, suspended from a garland of leaves, a cherub keeps watch over the child who slumbers in its cradle. The ever-watchful Gelert stands alert at the end of the crib and the very obviously dead wolf lies below them.

There should also be room in this collection for those figures of a purely decorative nature which may well have been aimed at the ever-growing numbers of English visitors who were discovering the delights of North Wales as tourists. They are an assortment of attractive, well coloured groups of farmers and their wives carrying their wares to market in baskets and other receptacles. Always with their distinctive dress, and the tall hats which the English probably assumed were everyday wear, some were inscribed 'Welch Shepherds' and even 'Welsh Hunters'. They depicted a rather idyllic, rural existence which could only be imagined by the potters in the smoke-laden, filthy conditions of the Potteries. They were very far from the truth, but they perpetuated a dream.

The popularity of Staffordshire figures in Wales shows an interesting continuity of taste which has survived well into this century. Apart from portrait figures, there has always been a strong affection for Staffordshire animals, and this strength of association is exemplified by one A. F. Tschiffely, a traveller who wrote in his book *This Way Southward*, of visiting the homesteads of Welsh settlers in Patagonia early in this century. 'During my visit . . . I almost invariably saw curious white china dogs on the mantelpieces.' No doubt he saw other figures too, figures which had a story to tell about the people and places left behind. Figures which still have a special place in many Welsh homes.

FURTHER READING

Staffordshire Portrait Figures by P. D. Gordon Pugh (Antique Collector's Club).

The Victorian Staffordshire Figure by Anthony Oliver (Heinemann).

Staffordshire Pottery – The Tribal Art of England by Anthony Oliver (Heinemann).

THE HISTORY OF WELSH PORCELAIN AT SWANSEA AND NANTGARW

Jim Lloyd

CERAMIC PRODUCTION IN VARIOUS FORMS can be traced back many centuries in Wales, whether made as domestic ware or for agricultural, industrial or constructional use. When referring to ceramics made for domestic use, it is surprising how many people unfamiliar with the method of its production often refer to it all in general terms as Welsh China. I have lost count of the number of occasions where people claim to possess 'a cupboard full of Swansea China' or a full service of Nantgarw China. This of course is hardly ever the case and suggests therefore that people do not know the difference between pottery and porcelain.

During the 17th and 18th centuries, china or porcelain was imported into Britain in great quantity mainly from China, Japan and latterly France and Germany. It was in great demand and considered superior to the earthenware items made at the various potteries throughout the country. Its distinguishing nature which made it so popular was its smooth quality and transparency which even the finest pottery did not possess.

It followed therefore that there was a need to experiment in the production of porcelain in this country and this was first achieved at the famous London factories of Bow and Chelsea in around 1740, other successes soon followed at Bristol, Derby, Longton Hall and Worcester. A small amount of experimental porcelain is known to have been made at the Cambrian Pottery, Swansea, under the ownership of George Haynes in around 1796, but this was of inferior quality having a distinct yellow tint within the body and certainly did not compare with what was to follow in South Wales in the next decade or so.

The story of Welsh porcelain really starts in one of those early English factories when a young, highly experienced and gifted porcelain decorator by the name of William Billingsley decided to leave the famous Derby factory where he had been trained as an artist and painter since the age of sixteen years – to set up a new factory in the village of Pinxton, Derbyshire, in 1796. He had been commissioned with this task by a rich and famous industrialist from the area by the name of John Coke of Brook Hill Hall. The factory was built near a canal at Pinxton, the business established and fine porcelain was made and decorated at these premises. Billingsley, however, was forced to sever his links with the factory after only three years due to the lack of financial reward.

He then worked for short periods at other factories in Derbyshire, Nottinghamshire and Worcester before moving with his two daughters and son-in-law Samuel Walker to the village of Nantgarw some half way between Cardiff and Pontypridd. That was in the autumn of 1813. Billingsley is however reported to have visited Swansea in around 1808 when seeking employment as a decorator at the famous Cambrian Pottery, but having failed to find work was forced to travel to Worcester, on foot, where he was given a position at the Worcester China factory. It may well be that it was during that early visit to South Wales that he first saw the potential of setting up business in the area.

At the time of arriving in Nantgarw, Billingsley had in his possession the grand sum of £250 with which to set up his business. He leased Nantgarw House from a local farmer and then set about preparing the first kiln for firing the porcelain inside the house. Having established this small factory, he first experimented with porcelain pastes with the aim of producing porcelain to rival the soft paste items manufactured at Serves in France and which already adorned most of the great houses in Europe.

A Swansea porcelain cruciform sauce tureen from the County Sligo service.
(Note dolphin finial).

His choice of location at Nantgarw for his factory is now rather obvious. There was at hand ample supply of good quality coal for firing the kilns with an equal abundance of clean and pure water. Land was inexpensive when compared with land in his native Derbyshire, and he had also recognised the advantage of a direct link with the Bristol Channel by means of the recently constructed Glamorgan Canal running close to his factory. This he would use to transport potting clay from the docks at Cardiff to his factory and the finished product could likewise be forwarded again to Cardiff for transportation to its final destination. Production could not be started immediately as there had to be some construction work in preparing the factory, moulds and equipment had to be acquired and experienced staff found.

Billingsley was of course familiar with the manufacture of porcelain as well as with its decoration in which he was without doubt one of the great masters. During his time at the Derby factory, he had been encouraged to experiment with others in producing different porcelain bodies and with the experience gained at other factories on his travels, there was little that he did not know by the time he arrived in South Wales.

Porcelain is either of hard paste or the soft paste variety and it is important to be able to distinguish between the two. When discussing Welsh Porcelain however one is referring always to the soft paste variety.

The paste of the Nantgarw Porcelain was Billingsley's own secret which no one has shared or been able to reproduce to this very day. We know briefly that it was achieved by fusing materials of glass with another mixture known as frit and the whole mixture was then blended with English Clay. That is really all we know about the recipe which was personally prepared by Billingsley or possibly entrusted to his son-in-law Samuel Walker. The softness, purity and extraordinary translucency of the finished article makes it equal to any of the finest porcelain produced anywhere in the world.

Unfortunately, however, in order to gain these properties and maintain the strict quality upon which Billingsley insisted, the amount of spoilt ware was considerable and is reported to have been as high as 90%. This resulted from pieces collapsing, cracking, melting and warping due mainly to the purity of the paste which proved so difficult to fire: even today, it is not easy to find upright pieces that are uniformly true and perfect in shape, as with close examination, evidence of some sagging or warping is more or less to be expected. This problem did not effect flatware to such an extent, but again, by holding the item level with the eye, unevenness along the edging is not unusual.

This inevitably led to financial difficulties for Billingsley and the £250 available to him when setting up the business soon vanished. He was then introduced to a well-known personality in the area by

the name of William Weston Young. He was a man of great skills
and vision who had moved to the Neath valley from Bristol and was
admired as an architect, marine salvager, brickmaker, farmer and
miller. He was also a gifted artist and painter. Once Young became
aware of the financial plight facing Billingsley and Walker, he
invested a substantial amount of his own money into the venture in
the hope of maintaining production and in time profitability. This,
however, proved not to have been the case and his contribution
was insufficient to allow production for much longer.

An application by Billingsley and others for Government
assistance to support the factory in line with other porcelain manu-
facturers in Europe was refused but led however to a visit to the
factory by a Sir Robert Banks, President of The Royal Society and a
member of the Government committee. He took with him Lewis
Weston Dillwyn, the then owner of the Cambrian Pottery factory at
Swansea, who was extremely impressed by what he saw within the
factory. Billingsley and Walker were soon persuaded to leave Nantgarw and to transfer their potters and their equipment to the
Cambrian site at Swansea. Indeed, they had little choice in the
matter, as without the financial support offered to them by Dillwyn
it is unlikely that they would ever have produced porcelain again.

This deal and the transfer was completed by the autumn of 1814.

Part of the equipment taken to Swansea were a number of porcelain
moulds which had been used at Nantgarw. Dillwyn had been
unable to acquire his own moulds during that early period and was
dependent therefore on those taken from Nantgarw to start production.

Porcelain was not immediately produced at Swansea as L. W.
Dillwyn – being a keen and shrewd businessman, doubted the
commercial value of the Nantgarw body in its present form –
insisted on further experimentation to discover a more reliable body
thus avoiding the financial loss experienced at Nantgarw. This was
in fact achieved under the supervision of Samuel Walker who was
placed in charge of these experimentations. By including bone ash

A collection of butter prints from the end of the nineteenth century, showing a variety of designs.

Photo: Robert Pugh Antiques/John Fry

A good beer jug from Sunderland, showing the trophies of the Navy. Note: the elaborate mend suggests that this jug has been treasured for a long time.

An oak 'tridarn' cupboard with a decorated middle door. Snowdonia, the end of the seventeenth century.

An oak dresser with open plate shelving, and drawers and cupboards in the bottom. Meirionethshire, mid-eighteenth century.

A London decorated Nantgarw trio *(left)*.
A Swansea 'glassy' porcelain cup and saucer *(right)*.

in the mix, much in line with the Derby and Worcester body. Although expensive to produce, it proved to have greater durability than the Nantgarw examples and was equally well received by its decorators, especially in London. This new body was indeed of exceptionally fine quality displaying a faint green translucency, what is now commonly known as duck egg porcelain.

With further experimenting, using soaprock mineral brought in from the Lizard peninsula, Cornwall, a more glassy type of porcelain was developed and produced, but for a short time only. Due to the slightly pitted finish of the glaze and the rather brownish translucency of the body this did not prove at all popular with the decorators. This type of porcelain did not contain any china clay and the finished item appears more like opaque glass than china. Such items are now, however, quite rare and most pieces are marked in colours of red, gold, green or puce in script. The decoration on glassy china found today is more likely to display evidence of wear and rubbing than the early duck egg variety. The well-known Swansea trident body was made in a similar way but proved even less popular with the London decorators.

The Swansea paste, now due to its improved strength and serviceability, allowed for greater variety of shapes and designs, especially in upright pieces, and follows therefore that a greater amount of Swansea China was produced and survived for collectors today. Large amounts of porcelain of outstanding quality was produced at Swansea between 1814 and 1817. The shapes, designs and decoration was indeed varied and included flatware, tureens, sucriers, comports, vases, pot pourri jars, candle holders and taper stands, cabinet cups and saucers, spill holders, ink wells, pen holders, and a variety of other items. Individually designed services were made for members of the Royal Family, heads of states, military leaders, large country houses and estates as well as other independently commissioned pieces through London and Bristol based agents representing these Welsh factories. One such agent who took personal interest in Swansea porcelain at the time was John Mortlock and Company, Oxford Street, London. Little, if any of this porcelain, was ever intended for the common man – the prices even then were well beyond what everyone but the very rich could afford. The only opportunity available to the poor and working-class to handle such items was possibly for someone in service within these great houses. Many of the items made were never meant for general use but only for display as cabinet pieces.

Billingsley appears not to have approved of the experimental work on the new porcelain body at Swansea and played no part in its development. He had a major disagreement with Dillwyn probably over the latter's interference and insistence in changing the nature of the paste. This resulted in Billingsley returning to Nantgarw in December 1816 or very early in 1817. This coincided with Dillwyn's retirement from the business and leasing the factory to his manager Timothy Bevington and his son John Bevington. Walker followed Billingsley to Nantgarw later in 1817 and porcelain production in Swansea continued only for a short time under Bevington's ownership.

Billingsley's intentions when setting up his business in Wales was to concentrate only on the production of fine porcelain and to leave

he decoration to the London based artists. This was despite the fact
nat he was himself recognised as the foremost decorator and painter,
specially of flowers in the country. He was also an accomplished
andscape artist and many of his early pieces, were of Derbyshire
cenes including some of the great country houses in that county.
Ie is today best remembered for his skill in painting roses in par-
cular, in a style which he developed by removing some of the colour
pplied to the porcelain with the use of a dry brush, thereby allowing
ne whiteness of the body to show through the colour and thereby
etermining the variety of soft and delicate shades required to make
ne petals as lifelike as possible. He painted his roses from various
ngles often showing views from below and behind the flower.

Another outstanding decorator working in the area at the time
vas one Thomas Pardoe, another of those great artists apprenticed
) the Derby works at a young age in the late 18th century and who
lso worked for a time at the Worcester factory before moving to
outh Wales around 1795 or 1796. His first engagement in Wales
vas as a decorator at the Cambrian Pottery, Swansea, and it was
uring his time at Swansea that he met and befriended the man
Villiam Weston Young whose antecedents we have already covered.
. similarity exists in the decorative work of these men especially in
andscape scenery and this is undoubtedly due to Young develop-
ng his skills through his association and friendship with Pardoe.
ndeed, both men are known to have lived together for a time
uring Pardoes' employment at the Cambrian pottery. Although
ardoes' work was in the main on pottery, he is known also to have
ecorated on porcelain and in particular on Nantgarw ware. He is
nown to have spent a great deal of time at the Nantgarw factory
etween 1820 and 1822 when he worked with William Weston Young
ecorating a stock of white, unfinished china acquired by Young when
roduction at Nantgarw ended in 1820. Pardoe is unlikely to have
ecorated any of the Swansea china however as he had already
noved to the Bristol area as a decorator and guilder before the start
f porcelain production at Swansea.

A locally decorated Swansea porcelain plate *(left)*.
Two fine London decorated Nantgarw plates *(centre and right)*.

Although a large majority of Swansea china was also sent to London to be decorated, a number of talented resident decorators worked within the Swansea factory and it is this local work that is most sought after today. Such artists included Thomas Baxter, David Evans, Henry Morris, William Pollard and one George Beddow who specialised mainly in landscape scenes. Pollards' work has special interest mainly because he was born in the Landore area of Swansea and was therefore a truly local artist. Many of the items decorated with botanical scenes, birds and butterflies are attributed to William Weston Young, but the rarest and most desired pieces are of course those painted by Billingsley himself. The work of the London based artists was of the best standard possible and is often intricate, especially in the fine guilding within cups and coffee cans. The quality of all this work has undoubtedly complemented the porcelain to make it so desirable to collectors world wide today. In contrast to the local artists at Swansea, however, all the decoration on Nantgarw Porcelain could only have been done by Billingsley and latterly Thomas Pardoe or by those London based artists, there is no ecord of any other artists having worked at that factory. Billingsley s known to have decorated some services for local friends and ssociates, but his work on Nantgarw china is indeed rare.

To those unfamiliar with Welsh porcelain, even if the decorator annot be identified through style and design, then as a rule of humb, many pieces decorated in London can often be identified by faint iridescent shadowy border surrounding the decoration. This s believed to have developed as a result of sea air affecting the white porcelain during its transportation by sea to the London artists. does, however, require a keen eye to recognise these tell tale signs which are certainly not present in locally decorated china and applies mainly to Nantgarw Porcelain pieces.

As with most rare commodities, copies and fakes have been pro- uced over the years, therefore great care should always be taken when purchasing Welsh porcelain. Marks should never be taken as guarantee to an items authenticity. Marks on Nantgarw Porcelain re in the main straightforward with the word Nantgarw impressed nder the glaze on the underside of the item. The way that the word is set out may vary in that it is sometimes hyphenated and ccompanied by the initials C.W. for china works. Some pieces dis- lay the word Nantgarw in red stencil and others in gold and black ettering painted onto the glaze. These I would treat with some sus- icion and would consider them as probable fakes. The impressed mark, however, is unlikely to appear on small items such as cups nd saucers but nearly always on flatware. If in doubt, it is always dvisable to obtain advice from an expert or at least someone who familiar with the item.

The marks on Swansea porcelain are far more varied and the encil print mark of Swansea over the glaze is quite common. The word Swansea is also often painted by the decorator in script on the nderside in a variety of colours – mainly red, green, puce or black, robably one of the main colours used in the decoration itself. hese marks are again applied over the glaze, and the same care hould be taken to have it properly identified before investing in the

item. The impressed mark Swansea or a trident mark is of course fa
more reliable and is unlikely therefore to have been faked.

Between 1814 and early 1817, during Billingsley's time at Swan
sea, no porcelain was produced at Nantgarw. Most of the mould
had been removed to the Swansea factory in the autumn of 1814 i
order to start the production at the Cambrian works. We now know
that Nantgarw moulds were used at Swansea during the early day
of production and some moulds based on pottery designs mad
made at the Pottery were also used during the early days of por
celain manufacture at Swansea. Because of the improved strengt
of the Swansea body, greater and more complicated designs an
shapes were made which meant new moulds being created for th
factory. A flower and scroll plate mould was designed for th
Swansea factory which produced plates similar but not identical t
those made in the original Nantgarw mould. Having decided t
leave Swansea in 1817 for reasons which we have already covered
Billingsley found that he was unable to reclaim all of his origina
Nantgarw moulds, and again, new stock had to be made in orde
that he could again continue production at Nantgarw.

For the following 18 months or so, a substantial amount of fin
porcelain was produced at the Nantgarw factory due to the financi
support given to Billingsley by a number of wealthy and eminer
businessmen from the South Wales area. This is likely to have bee
the prime period when the finest items were made. The failure i
firing and wastage however remained high and the financial sup
port given to Billingsley proved insufficient to maintain productio
at the factory. This resulted in Billingsley and Walker having t
leave Nantgarw without warning in the spring of 1820, sadly takin
with them the sacred recipe of their wonderful porcelain.

The factory, the various moulds and equipment, together wit
a quantity of undecorated china were all calimed by William Westc
Young, a man who had been connected with the factory througho
its short history and who had done so much to help finance th
whole venture. He did not produce any porcelain of his own aft

acquiring the factory, but he was able to ensure that all the unfinished china purchased with the factory was decorated to a high standard. Fortunately, he managed to secure the service of one of the foremost decorators of the time, that of his close friend and one time colleague – Thomas Pardoe. The quality of painting on the items decorated by Pardoe between the years 1820 and 1822 is outstanding and unequal to anything I have seen on Nantgarw china. Pardoe died at Nantgarw in July 1823, his death being the closing chapter in the short but significant history of Welsh porcelain production. The factory remained in the Pardoe family for many years, but producing mainly clay pipes and other earthenware items.

Although porcelain and its production was in a way alien to our way of life in South Wales in the early years of the nineteenth century, and the people involved in its creation were all from outside Wales we must however be justly proud of that period in our history and even prouder of the fact that we were able to put our names to such superb porcelain which is so highly regarded by those fortunate enough to own it.

Anyone interested in researching the subject further are advised to visit their local reference libraries where they can have access to such books as *Nantgarw Porcelain* by W. D. John, *The Pottery and Porcelain of Swansea and Nantgarw* by E. Morton Nance, *Nantgarw Porcelain* by Rowland Williams and *The Ceramics of Swansea and Nantgarw* by William Turner. The reader is further advised to visit the National Museum of Wales, Cardiff, The Glynn Vivian Art Gallery, Swansea, or the Merthyr Tydfil Museum at Cyfarthfa Castle where so much of this wonderful china can be viewed. In conclusion, although items of Nantgarw and Swansea porcelain are indeed rare and therefore commanding high prices generally, there are still sufficient pieces available for those serious drivers who may decide to start his or her own collection.

WELSH LOVE SPOONS

Carol Pugh

IT IS HARD TO IMAGINE, when one surveys today's cheap, mass-produced sentimentality that there was a time when such tokens of affection were the result of hours of unpaid, often highly skilled work, sometimes undertaken in poor light and uncomfortable conditions.

Rustic swains with their hearts set on a comely milk-maid would be unlikely to have the wherewithal for, nor access to, the more obvious forms of loving gift. So they turned to something close to hand and fashioned from whatever material was available, to the best of their very variable skills, tokens of love in the form of small personal items such as knitting sheathes, stay busks, and lace bobbins. But the token which seems to have turned the heads and stirred the hearts most of all still carries with it a romantic tradition which is hard to resist – the Welsh love spoon.

Why the Welsh made the love-spoon their own is not apparent but other examples of similar traditions also evolved regionally. Knitting sheathes predominated in the sheep-keeping areas of the Northern counties of Britain and the borders where the tradition of knitting had drifted across the border from Scotland. These particular examples of hand-made love tokens however also had served some useful purpose; all but the most simplistic form of love-spoon were quite unsuitable for supping soup! There also appears to have been a tradition of spoons as love tokens in Scandinavian countries, but it is predominantly with Wales that we associate the tradition in Great Britain.

Inevitably the first question to be addressed is the most obvious -

why spoons? The humble spoon has been for centuries one the most familiar items of household equipment and the practise of storing spoons, fitting snugly together as they do, prompted the adoption, during 18th century, of the delightfully descriptive adjective 'spoonways' whose imaginative use eventually embraced the human desire to emulate the closeness of these spoons, ultimately as in the marital bed. The word's romantic associations developed apace and, in time, our prim Victorian ancestors adopted the verb 'to spoon' to describe the courting process. Indeed, it remained in general usage well into the 20th century.

Like so many rural crafts, it is difficult to be precise as to the origins of love spoons in terms of date. Fortunately for today's collectors sufficient numbers survive inscribed with a date to enable us to trace the styles, in as far as one can with such objects. One of the earliest recorded shows a date of 1667. Most of the spoons which come onto the market today date from the late 18th and 19th centuries. However, styles and designs would have been copied by generations of spoon carvers, so dating is not a very precise science and indeed, it does not need to be. And if those spoons with a broad, flat pierced handle seem to come predominantly from North Wales, while those which display clumsy carving and a lack of pro-portion tend to derive from Pembrokeshire, it is of little consequence compared to their value to the fortunate recipient. What is certain is that such prized possessions would have been displayed in a place of honour and no doubt the most eligible lasses could acquire a small collection of these spoons before choosing her mate.

The infinite variety of styles and design found in Welsh love spoons mean that there are rarely two the same. Their great charm is, there-fore, what they represent and a close study reveals a fascinating lesson in symbolism. All this symbolism translates into a serious declaration of devotion and one must look closely at these emblems to interpret the messages so eloquently composed in love spoons.

Spoons were carved and whittled from the most accessible and workable materials to hand. Thus a great variety of woods are found,

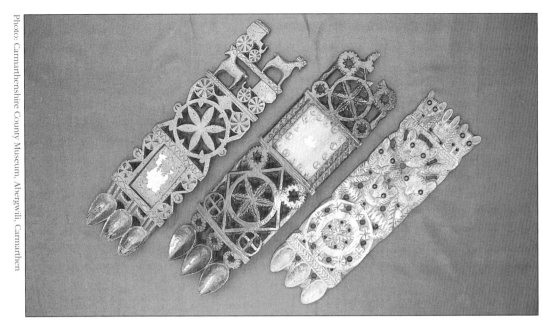

Three particularly fine and rare Welsh love spoons.

but the easily worked sycamore and fruitwoods are common. Deceptively simple is a spoon illustrated in colour, the size of a small teaspoon and made from a piece of mutton bone, scratch-carved with a picture of a sheep. Occasionally use of a foreign wood, such as mahogany, suggests the work of a sailor, as does carved whale-bone or ivory, and the additional embellishment of inlaid coloured wax or tiny brass pins. Spoon handles frequently incorporate a lantern or cage containing free-moving balls which seems simply to have demonstrated the skill of the carver. However, the regularity with which this particular technicality appears in love spoons causes one to wonder whether the technique, once mastered, was in fact deceptively simple. The skill of some of these spoon-makers knew no bounds and they were soon incorporating knives and forks in their repertoire, along with swivels and chains, and a turning wheel has been recorded which perhaps relates to the donor's occupation, or just his willingness to work.

While the intensely personal nature of these gifts was of immense importance, there is no doubt that not everyone had the dexterity to produce even the most basic spoon, and it is probable that anyone

Photo: Carmarthenshire County Museum, Abergwili, Carmarthen

with a talent for carving could put this skill to profitable purpose by supplying others. This could also account for the similarity in designs in certain areas. In fact, towards the end of the 19th century the genteel Victorians produced sugar tongs commercially, decorated with chip-carving and a window for a written name and date.

The techniques employed in the making of love spoons were naturally limited by the materials and tools available, but quite sophisticated three dimensional carving is found on the more elaborate spoon handles and further decoration was applied with chip or scratch carving. Whereas the experienced eye may eventually be able to identify regional characteristics in spoons, familiar nautical emblems such as ships, anchors, chains, knots or even dolphins make sailors' spoons easy to identify. Some spoons are deceptively simple in their execution, others bewildering in their complexity; but all carry a similar message in its symbols and motifs.

The most common motif, the heart, is self-evident and where two hearts are entwined no further explanation is need from me! Closely associated with the heart, and almost as common, is a device which looks like a rather fat comma. This symbol comes with all the mystical powers of ancient Egypt, for it is their sign for 'the soul'. Thus hearts and commas declare 'heart and soul'. Keyholes were another powerful device offering the way into the suitors' heart – and home, as they sometimes appear with a small house, and even occasionally a key! So now the message is becoming clear. 'Come live with me and be my love!'

However, the formalities still must be observed and while many love spoons incorporating intricate chains were no doubt a demonstration of the carver's skill, perhaps they also indicated a willingness to be bound by the chains that bind a marriage.

Shoes and boots (still associated today with wedding traditions) appear frequently on love spoons and the origins of this message come, not surprisingly, from a reference in the Bible where the exchange of a shoe signified agreement of a contract (marriages often being arranged by way of a business contract in Old Testament days).

Initials are frequently in incorporated with or without dates, and one regularly sees spoons with a deeper, oblong window cut out into which is inserted a piece of paper inscribed with names and dates. One cannot help wondering whether this was to enable the canny suitor to keep all his options open. Rejected by one maid, it would then be a simple matter to replace the paper with the name of someone else. Similar insertions of mirror are also occasionally found. The significance of this is not clear. Maybe it was just a shard which added bright decoration to the humble spoon; it was rarely large enough to serve as a looking glass. Or perhaps old super-stitions died hard in the country, for the mirror was powerful magic against the evil eye and all its associated ill luck.

So far, so good. The declaration has been made and hopefully the message, so painstakingly and laboriously carved into the handle of the love spoon, is loud and clear. We then come to the bowl of the spoon which, compared to the intricacies of decoration which has preceded it, remained remarkably simple and unadorned. Some-times the spoon will terminate in two bowls, side by side like man and wife. On rare occasions multiple spoon bowls are carved in the piece predicting the hoped-for family which will result from such a union.

Nowadays, love spoons command a relatively high price on both sides of the Atlantic, it would be easy to confer on them academic importance very far from their humble origins. Therefore, it behoves us to remember the intensely personal nature of the giving of a love spoon; often simply an overture to a declaration of love, or a com-memoration of a betrothal, marriage, anniversary, or birth. And that, by and large, they were given to and by illiterate, inarticulate country dwellers, and almost exclusively in Wales. But they contained a power-ful message in their strong symbolism. An offer of love, devotion and hope for the future, made unreservedly and for ever. It was powerful and heady stuff to those who, although unable to read the written word, knew the content of the message given and received.

TREEN
Domestic items made of wood

Robert Pugh

TREEN AS A COLLECTING FIELD is very difficult to define and means different things to different people. It is the generic term for domestic artefacts fashioned from wood – literally 'of a tree'. In his monumental work on the subject Edward Pinto took the very broad view that treen described any small item made of wood, embracing fairly large boxes as well as Tunbridgeware within his definition.

In Wales we tend to think more along the lines of rural artefacts, particularly those associated with the kitchen and dairy. It is these practical, everyday objects from the cottage, rather than smart items from the big house, which we intend to cover here. The woods from which these objects were made was mostly sycamore, oak, elm, fruitwoods, and pine. Each has its own characteristics which make them suitable for different purposes and bestows on them their visual appeal by means of their colour and grain.

Sycamore is a tight-grained, but fairly soft, wood which makes it particularly easy to keep clean. Furthermore, it does not tend to have knots, nor does it splinter when scrubbed. Therefore, for reasons of hygiene, it lends itself to be used for items that are directly in touch with food, such as butter workers and dairy bowls. Sycamore is also very soft, which makes it ideal for carving and turning, and thus its common application in the making of butter prints. However, this soft, sweet wood also makes it the perfect target for woodworm, to which it is much prone. More commonly

71

used for smaller items, cricket tables and even big farmhouse tables are sometimes found with sycamore tops. When scrubbed they develop a wonderful pale, creamy colour.

Oak is a wood better associated with country furniture than small objects, but the very term 'Welsh oak' seems to add to an article's desirability. Although naturally pale in colour, oak acquires the most wonderful dark patination with age, use and, most importantly, regular polish. Apart from major pieces of furniture, many smaller items were made in oak. A hard wood, it probably survived better than some of the softer woods mentioned here, and was commonly used for such Welsh domestic objects as spoon racks, salt boxes and candle boxes.

Elm, and its very similar cousin ash, are used in much the same way as oak and are preferred by some enthusiasts because of their slightly lighter, warmer colours and distinctive grain. These woods would have been put to similar use as oak, but other treen items such as bread peels are also found in elm.

Fruitwoods demand little explanation. Soft and easily worked, they would have been used simply for reasons of economy and availability. Probably not used as widely in Wales as in England, their beauty lies in their richness and variety of colour.

Pine was traditionally used in poorer homes, both for furniture as well as smaller artefacts. Initially, pine was almost invariably painted. For many years it was the fashion to strip the paint and polish the raw pine in a manner that was never originally intended. Now, collectors, and even those magazines whose obsession with 'stripped pine' caused the trouble in the first place, are realising that the most desirable finish of all is that of the original paint. Often this original layer of paint is the hardest and can be retained when those over it are carefully scraped off. This has to be done dry (causing the item much less harm than immersion into a caustic soda tank), and is called dry scraping. It is a much more skilled business than one might think and should only be undertaken after taking advice.

Spoon Racks are found in any of the above mentioned woods. In Wales they are of stepped form, made up of two, three, or even four tiers. This is because Welsh country spoon racks are made to hold round-handled, sycamore *cawl* spoons, not the pewter flat-handled spoons which flat-backed, English spoon racks were designed to take. As with all items of treen, the points to look for are originality, colour and detail of adornment. Welsh spoon racks often incorporate pierced decoration to the back board or front apron, with traditional motifs such as hearts.

Cawl **Spoons** were once common in most country sales and antiques shops, but are now becoming very scarce and have taken on a desirability quite out of proportion to their intrinsic value. Part of this problem is that the collector is likely to need upwards of fifteen spoons to fill his rack. By their very nature, of course, they would have been discarded at the end of their useful life, were easily damaged or simply lost along the way. Spoons differ considerably

Mid 19th century Welsh oak spoon rack with cawl spoons.

from area to area, some having almost round bowls and some being
the shape of a rugby ball. Handles vary enormously, some being
cylindrical with simple turning, others squared and tapering to a
point.

Candle Boxes were very simply made objects, more often than
not in oak, but sometimes in pine, with a bevelled, sliding lid that
lifted upwards when the box was hung on the wall. Candles were a
precious commodity, especially in poor, rural districts. Similarly
rushlight boxes were made to accommodate this cheaper form of
lighting, but these were open topped and the rushlights stood in
them like spills.

Rushlight Holders represented the very poorest form of domestic
lighting at a time when candles were a luxury. The rushlights them
selves were prepared by cutting rushes in autumn, soaking them in
water, then drying them in the sun. Afterwards they were peeled
almost back to the pith and dipped in animal fat in a grissett (a
long-handled, iron boat-shaped utensil), to form a long, thin, crude
candle. These burned relatively quickly, so they were held in a
metal holder fixed into a wooden base. The holder was a simple
weighted clamp, often incorporating a candlestick as well, thus
enabling the rushlight to be adjusted very easily. Some have very
crude square cut wooden bases while eighteenth century example
have finer turned bases, often conical in shape. Floor standing ex
amples are also found.

The very simple construction of rushlight holders makes it par
ticularly difficult to ascertain whether or not they are old, and if so
how old. They were made and used over a very long period in
country districts and the problem of authentication is accentuated
because they now realise the sort of prices which makes faking
them a financially rewarding occupation.

Stone Boxes were an essential item for the country kitchen

Photo: © Richard Bebb, Country Antiques (Wales)

A pine skew with high back;
west Wales, nineteenth
century.

A striped red and white
quilt with exceptional
embroidery, which won a
best quilt competition in
Llanelli in 1901.

A large pinwheel quilt
in dark blue and red;
intricate embroidery:
Cardiganshire, 1875.

Edward Morgan and Jenny Jones –
romantic figures of their time.

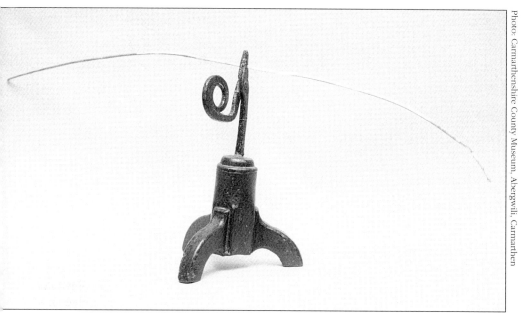

A rare 18th century rushlight holder.

Photo: Carmarthenshire County Museum, Abergwili, Carmarthen

heir function was to clean knives and keep them sharp. They onsist of a flat plank some two feet six inches to three feet long ith a simple, open box at the bottom which held a piece of Bath one. The stone was used on the knife which was then rubbed on ie long upright of the box. Stone boxes are generally made of pine nd in the twentieth century similar devices were developed with a ather 'board' fulfilling the same purpose.

Breadboards or Planks would have been found in every home nd many survive, and indeed some are still in use. The best and irliest Welsh breadboards were large and round (14-16 inches in iameter). Cut from a single plank they have a shaped tailpiece ierced with a hole by which they were hung. These were made of rcamore, pine, or even occasionally teak. (Teak was also some-mes used in West Wales for cricket table tops, the wood probably oming from the shipyards). Later breadboards are about a foot in ameter, often carved with corn heads around the edge, and some-nes the word 'BREAD'.

Bread Peels are flat 'spades' with long handles used for removing bread from the oven after baking. Most commonly made from sycamore or elm, they have a tapered leading edge with which to lift the loaf from the floor of the oven. These simple utensils are popular decoration for modern-day kitchens, no doubt because they are invariably pleasing in shape and of good colour.

Butter Prints are one of the most prolific items of treen and also one of the most sought-after. Found all over Wales, they are usually made of sycamore and vary enormously in their decoration. The conscientious dairy-maid would have kept her butter prints under water in the dairy, so that in use the damp print would not adhere to the butter and would leave a crisp imprint in it. Thus, old butter prints are often found with splits where the wood has dried out.

The most common design, and yet one of the most desirable is, for obvious reasons, the cow. Other common patterns include roses, thistles, acorns and the Prince of Wales feathers. Most butter prints are plain, circular prints incorporating a wooden knob handle and were simply used to mark the butter pat. Sometimes they are enclosed within a cup, which also acts as a measure for the butter with the print pushing through to both mark and eject the butter in one action. Another variety is the roller print which has a wheel and handle and simply repeats its pattern around the butter, probably in a big tub.

Three-dimensional butter prints, or butter moulds were also made with two opposing halves held together by wooden pins. The variety of these is considerable as they were often used for exhibition or display purposes. The most commonly found is a swan.

Although used widely throughout Britain, butter prints are prolific in Wales, and the boat-shaped variety is traditionally thought of as Welsh. The illustrated example is rare in that it incorporates the name of the dairy, and the cupped print bears the name of its farm *Tyn Llan.*

An interesting domestic set of very small butter prints (appro:

1½") were recently seen by the author, carved with a coat of arms and the day of the week – quite a useful affectation at breakfast should one be lucky enough to live such a life of Riley!

There is one word of warning to the aspiring butter print collector. Traditionally they tend to be described as Victorian. Indeed many of them are, but many elderly people will remember them in use. Although it makes little difference to their appeal or their value, it should be remembered that most of those we see are, in fact, probably twentieth century.

Dairy Bowls are one of the most attractive items of Welsh treen. They seem to be found only rarely now and condition is very important. They are usually of sycamore which, from years of use, has often mellowed to a wonderful colour. However, there are two dangers – woodworm and splitting. Sometimes this latter problem has resulted in the bowl being rivetted many years ago, and this kind of 'mend' sometimes has an appeal of its own. Ideally, however, bowls should be perfect with a couple of simple turned lines on the outside and a good, thick, flat rim. The last criterion – big is beautiful, and huge is more beautiful still.

Platters and Trenchers are both posh names for plates. Although humble, everyday objects, they are keenly sought by collectors of treen. Like spoons, their very familiarity seems to have resulted in their scarcity today. Precious china plates were at least decorative, but there was little use for the humble wooden plate once it became damaged, stained, or perhaps scarred by burning and, lacking the dignity of larger items of treen, they were simply thrown away.

The earliest and best examples of trenchers are square, with a circular indented central area and a small indentation for salt in the flat area on one corner. Later examples are simple, round plates slightly larger than a tea-plate. Again sycamore was the most suitable material, and in use regular scrubbing would result in a pale, clean surface. Collectors now like to polish these little plates, and they make a fine display on a dresser in their understated, simple way.

The desirability of trenchers has led, as in so many other fields of collecting, to reproductions or even true fakes appearing on the market. However, time is on the side of the collector in this. All plates would have been turned and thus have started life perfectly circular. Only age and the grain of the wood can bring them to a very slightly oval shape – and this is something which cannot be faked.

Butter Scales or Dairy Scales, traditionally used in the dairy, took the form of a very simple wooden balance. Made of oak, pine or sycamore (or any combination of these), they usually had beech or sycamore pans suspended on string! The principle was that weights were not used, but a sample pat of butter was created, by separate weighing or from a mould, and used in place of a weight. The process then became self-perpetuating.

Butter Workers included an assortment of tools which were used to work the butter in the final stages after churning. The most important of these were butter 'hands' and the flat, circular presses which also served as a small, hand-held working table. With the press in one hand holding the butter, it could then be worked into shape with a butter 'hand'. Smaller versions of these presses were probably more often used for squeezing excess water out of the butter.

The rarest form of butter scoops.
Late 19th century.

'Hands' come in various sizes. The are paddle-shaped, generally with a rectangular blade and an oval handle. Some are rounded on their back, giving them extra weight, and all are ribbed on their working surface.

In the kitchen, rather than in the dairy, would be found small, sycamore half-circular bladed butter curlers, sometimes with a serrated edge, and occasionally with a little butter print carved into the handle. Butter scoops also were made from sycamore. A broad, slightly dished scoop on the end of a short, stout handle which, again, could be topped with a roundel incised with some decorative motif for imprinting on the butter.

HORN AND ITS DOMESTIC USES

From time immemorial the horns of animals have always been admired both for their shape and for the uses to which they can be put. Very large horns have always been a source of wonderment and in ancient times were used by kings and chieftains as ceremonial vessels and status symbols. As late as the nineteenth century the horns of the champion Durham ox, a vast creature recorded in prints and on blue and white pottery, were regarded as a spectacle and even went on tour! They were displayed in Cardiff at the Three Tuns Inn.

The availability of horn in rural areas made it a natural material for domestic items of both a decorative and a purely practical nature. Surprisingly malleable when heated, horn could be flattened or even have its colour changed. Thus, pieces of horn were pressed as thinly as possible resulting in a translucent panel which could be used in lanterns ('lanthorns'). It could also be pressed and moulded in such a way as to accept a pattern of considerable complexity.

The kind of horn items which are likely to be found in Wales tend to be the work-a-day pieces which were used extensively in everyday domestic use. Simple beakers were often cut from the sections of horns and were used everyday. It was not uncommon for them to be decorated with incised 'engraving', often rather crudely, but sometimes in a surprisingly sophisticated manner. Engravings ranged from initials and dates or familiar domestic items, through to lively hunting scenes running around the body of the beaker. Inevitably, it is these decorated examples that are of most interest to today's collector.

Snuff boxes were made, mainly in North Wales, sometimes with inscriptions giving the name of the owner, in much the same way that miners' chewing tobacco boxes were used in the south. In the century or more since they were made these boxes have tended to warp slightly and lids are now often ill-fitting. In Scotland much more formal use was made of horn for snuff boxes, or mulls, which could be highly elaborate affairs made from whole horns, highly polished and even silver-mounted.

Meanwhile, in a domestic, or agricultural situation, the natural vessel-shape offered by the horn lent itself to countless uses. Apart from the traditional uses as sounding horns and powder horns sand and tallow were also carried about in them for use in the field for sharpening scythes. Seeds, too, were both carried and distributed from horns. Some of those most often seen give little clue as to their purpose, but were likely to have been used for drenching animals that is applying medicine straight down their throats.

It was obviously important that these various uses of horns should be kept specifically for their intended purpose. In fact, each type would have a slightly different angle on the cut end (the spout) so that grease from a grease horn would flow differently to the oil based medicines from a drenching horn. Thus, although many horns look basically the same, it is important for the collector to learn the specific differences between them. For instance, a particularly unusual and specialist use for a horn was as a thumb shield for protecting the thumb when removing bark from trees for use in the tanning industry, but such an item would not be easily recognised by the layman.

NINETEENTH CENTURY LUSTRE POTTERY

Robert Pugh

LUSTREWARE POTTERY has always been close to the Welsh heart, whether or not it was made in Wales. These metallic glazes that can make humble pieces of pottery look like burnished metal have been used for many hundreds of years in Islamic poteries but in a British context the technique goes back only to the latter part of the eighteenth century and was not produced in commercial quantities until the early part of the 19th.

There is a much quoted letter written to the Staffordshire Mercury in 1846 by John Hancock claiming to be the man who invented lustreware while working for Spode in 1789. In any event, silver and pink were in use during the first decade of the nineteenth century, and copper by the 1830s.

There are three main varieties of lustreware which we will consider here. The terms used to describe them are deceptive and so should be sorted out without further ado. The metallic compound which gives rise to the lustre is not necessarily that which the finished piece of pottery resembles.

Thus silver lustre is based on platinum, which does not tarnish and retains a high silvery sheen, silver itself would tarnish and fail to shine. Platinum lustre is generally used on a dark body when completely covering items to make them look like silver. When used for silver 'resist' items it is usually on a light body.

Copper lustre is derived from gold for similar reasons, but here a further complication arises in that pink lustre too uses gold as its base. The different finishes are partly due to the density of the

Three items of copper lustre from the mid 19th century.

lustering, but more importantly to the colour underneath the metalli
glaze. This background colour may be the 'body' colour (i.e. th
colour of the clay), or it might be coloured glaze. Therefore, 'golc
lustre put onto a white background will result in a slightly metalli
bright pink, whereas on a dark base it will become copper lustre
Variations on this theme give rise to further lustre finishes, fo
instance a 'gold' lustre over a blue body or glaze will result in a
attractive purple metallic appearance.

Iron too was used and produced a thin, bright orange lustre use
mainly for decorating the edges of items or for highlighting. Thi
technique is usually referred to as 'tinselling'. This was a techniqu
used on Swansea Pottery but only very late on in the factory's life
in the period of D. J. Evans. The most noteworthy example bein
the rims of 'Birds' pattern jugs.

In summary:

      Gold on white background   =   pink lustre
      Gold on a dark ground   =   copper lustre

| Platinum | = | silver lustre |
| Iron | = | orange lustre ('tinselling') |

From here on we will refer to the colours by their appearance rather than their metal content, i.e. Pink, Silver and Copper.

The formula for preparing the lustre 'mix' varied, but in principle powdered metal was dissolved into a mixture of hydrochloric and nitric acids, and this in turn mixed with turpentine and linseed oil.

The technique of lustre decorating was largely applied to 'hollow ware', i.e. jugs, mugs, vases etc. and it is this application which is largely under discussion here. Occasionally, however early 19th century pottery figures were decorated with pink lustre (notably figures representing the Four Seasons), and at about the same time a variety of classical figures and animals in an all-over silver lustre glaze were also being made. Pink lustre mugs containing grotesque frogs were a popular early 19th century amusement, and rather later, pairs of spaniels were produced in Staffordshire in all-over copper lustre, but these lacked the detail and character of their cheerful, painted cousins.

PINK LUSTRE

Although many factories used pink lustre it would appear from an advertisement put out by the London warehouse of the Cambrian Pottery, Swansea, in 1807, that Swansea was among the very first factories to produce it commercially. The earliest example is probably the Chinese-influence mug illustrated by Morton Nance, but soon afterwards the typical Swansea pierced-border plates with simple views of cottages appeared. This series also gave rise to some of the most sought-after Swansea lustreware – similar pierced plates decorated with animals and birds.

The Cambrian pottery cow creamers of 1820-30 were also decorated with splashes of pink lustre and very rare examples show an entirely pink lustre cow standing on a green, grassy base – a particularly striking combination.

The other main centres for the production of pink lustre in the 1830's are Newcastle and Sunderland. Their large jugs, probably made more for presentation than use, are a familiar sight and their sheer scale gives them a presence which makes them highly desirable. They show many different transfer-printed views and verses the most common being the view of the bridge over the River Wear and ditties relating to the sweethearts of departing and returning sailors. Their famous plaques also provide an interesting field to the collector of pink lustre, with their variety of ship prints and a wealth of religious mottos.

Needless to say, Staffordshire was another major centre of production where over 250 small, and not so small, potteries used some sort of lustre decoration.

SILVER LUSTRE

Silver lustre was used in three distinct ways. It could either be used as additional decoration applied with a brush, in the same way as colours, or it could be used like a glaze all over an item (often of elaborate shape and moulding) to imitate silverware. The third and perhaps most interesting for a ceramic collector is the technique of silver resist.

The first two methods are self explanatory. However, the technique of silver resist decoration deserves further explanation. The idea was to create a background of silver lustre against which another form of decoration could be applied. Thus, the area intended *not* to be silver was painted with a mixture of glycerine and honey, or sometimes shellac, so that the item could then be entirely covered in the silver lustre 'mix'. When the item was fired the resisting material would be burned off leaving the area it had covered undecorated. Thus either the 'resist' area left was white (perhaps in a geometric

An unusual silver lustre sugar bowl, c.1840.

attern or in the shape of a bird), or the 'resist' area had been laid
ver a previously applied decoration (hand-painted or transfer-
rinted) which would be revealed in firing surrounded by silver. It
; these items, which show so well the contrast between the silver
background' and the underlying colour, which have always been
host treasured by collectors.

Sadly, although Swansea did use all sorts of lustre techniques, it
ow seems likely that the wonderful hunting jugs in silver resist and
lue transfer, which Nance believed to be the products of Swansea,
rere in fact made in Staffordshire.

COPPER LUSTRE

opper lustre pottery has been popular in Wales from the time it
as first made and is as popular amongst Welsh antiques collectors
ow as it ever was. This relationship between Wales and copper lustre
so ingrained that many people, not least English auctioneers,

actually refer to it as Welsh lustre. Many believe that copper lustr
was made to go on Welsh dressers. Conversely, it could be argue
that Welsh dressers were made to house copper lustre! They g
together like the proverbial horse and carriage. However, th
dresser did of course have a head start on copper lustre and woul
originally have housed early pottery plates – probably delft or, mor
likely, pewter.

Knowing of this great demand for copper lustre in their hom
market, it seems most strange that the Welsh potteries did no
produce it. This becomes even more curious when one conside
that both the Cambrian and Llanelly Potteries showed that the
were capable of producing copper lustre at the height of i
popularity, but chose to do so in only the most minute quantities.

The only known items of copper lustre produced in Swanse
are a small number of Dillwyn's Etruscanware 'Oinochoe' or jug
Etruscanware was made from a terracotta clay (found on th
Penllergaer estate which was owned by Dillwyn's brother) and s
this was the only time that the factory used a body suitable to tak
the copper lustre glaze. These were by necessity unmarked, as th
copper lustre glaze covers their base, and can only be identified h
their shape.

This question of identification is a problem common to virtual
all copper lustre. The lustre glaze invariable covers the base of th
items and would therefore have filled and obliterated any impre
sed mark. Equally, the finish did not lend itself to transfer-printe
marks. Interestingly, despite their very low out-put of copper-lustr
the South Wales Pottery at Llanelli came up with an ingeniou
solution to this problem. Curious clock-face jugs are sometimes (b
rather rarely) found and instead of the clock maker's name on th
face of the clock one finds the name of the proprietor of the facto
William Chambers Jnr. Similar clock-face jugs are found from oth
factories and sometimes marked with another maker's mar
However, if they do not bear Chambers' name they are not Llanelly

Although there are no other known pieces of Llanelly copp

Photo: Carmarthenshire County Museum, Abergwili, Carmarthen

A Llanelly Pottery copper lustre jug with a view of Neath Abbey.
The reverse side shows a clock-face marked William Chambers Jnr.

stre as such, from time to time one finds elaborately moulded jugs
ith running stags. A very similar mould is known to have been
sed at Llanelli for plain blue jugs but is certainly not unique to that
ctory. Local examples of these blue jugs usually bear an impres-
·d mark (SOUTH WALES POTTERY) on the foot rim. The blue
anelly examples have an applied foot, that is to say the foot of the
g is made separately and fixed to the jug. All the copper lustre
·amples I have seen are molded in one piece and thus can be
fely said not to be from Llanelly.

The collecting of copper lustre has one peculiar trait. Once one
is established that the item is copper lustre, that is to say it has an
opreciable amount of copper colour, then the secret is to have no
ore space wasted on the metallic colour but rather the space is best
led with as elaborate a decoration as possible. This decoration

manifests itself in many of the styles used to decorate other potter of the time. Rural scenes hand-painted in coloured enamels, transfer printing, applied mouldings of flowers and animals all appear regu larly, as well as bands of a rough, granular 'pebble-dashed' finish Pink lustre was also applied as a decorative contrast.

Most copper lustre was made in Staffordshire but a large pro portion was always destined for the Welsh market.

One word of warning. Copper lustre was made from the 1830 right through into the twentieth century. Many common styles ar found but it is important to look for the earlier examples with reall high lustre finish and good quality decoration. Lustre generally doe not lend itself to restoration, so good condition is of paramour importance. Better by far one good, perfect piece than half a doze 'dancing ladies' jugs!

FURNISHING THE WELSH HOME

Richard Bebb

WHEN ELIZABETH MORRIS of Llandre, Llanfrynach married in 1834, her dowry included a large chest with drawers, in which to keep her six blankets and six quilts. Priced at 7.10.0 it must have been an impressive piece, no doubt made of solid oak and perhaps decorated with her initials. Such a chest, with lift-up lid, would today be less desirable than a similar piece of furniture which has opening doors above the drawers. The latter was once very common in the homes of west Wales, and is universally known as the 'Carmarthen coffer'. Other pieces are so distinctive that they are still known by their Welsh terms in the English language – the 'cwpwrdd tridarn', the 'cwpwrdd deuddarn' and the 'coffor bach'.

THE CRAFTSMEN

Not only are these styles distinctive, each item is unique and it is very rare to find two which are quite the same. They were made by craftsmen who lived in the same communities as their customers and who understood perfectly their particular requirements. Many of them were in fact themselves part-time farmers, with holdings too small to support a family without another source of income. Some furniture makers made their main living producing other wooden objects such as wheels, barrels and even boats. The techniques they used in these occupations often led to distinctive ways of making chairs, cupboards and tables.

Books on furniture frequently distinguish between 'joiners', 'carpenters' and 'cabinet-makers', but such terms were interchangeable
in Wales. In Caernarfon in 1685 for example, William Bowen called
himself 'carpenter' in May, and 'wheelwright' in September, and in
the following year Griffith Evan was a 'carpenter' in April and a
'joyner' in September. Such men were very adaptable and often
combined a number of skills such as joinery, turning, and carving
which in English cities would have been performed by separate
groups. It is this mixture of techniques which makes so much of our
furniture individual and original.

Photo: © Richard Bebb, Country Antiques (Wales)

Traditional cricket table with a scrubbed sycamore top over a painted
ash base with an undertier, signed by Daniel Howells,
who made it in North Pembrokeshire in 1898.

Using mainly local timber, often felled on their customers' farms, the furniture they produced was expected to be durable. Some pieces were strictly utilitarian, like the thousands of small stools and round tables which were required by practically every home, and their design remained unchanged for centuries. But it is quite unusual for Welsh furniture to be completely plain. Even quite basic pieces have the odd decorative flourish which proclaim the pride of the craftsman in his work, and the value attached to the piece by the new owner. And some pieces are very decorative, and although made for quite small houses show the importance attached to the home and to important family occasions, especially marriages.

THE DRESSER

So distinctive are the dressers found in Wales, so varied and of such high quality, that the term 'Welsh dresser' has been used by the furniture trade as a generic term for over a hundred years. Virtually every rural house had one as a focal point of the main living room, and as industrialisation spread in the nineteenth century, the fashion was kept alive in the new settlements in the Valleys.

Developed from simple arrangements of shelves over work surfaces used in kitchens and dairies, the dresser took on quite elaborate forms and became the most treasured item in many families. It was handed down the generations, often in the female line, and became covered in family mementoes and pictures, as well as colourful plates, jugs and ornaments.

It evolved different styles in different localities, according to the abilities and inspiration of the local craftsmen, and the tastes and requirements of their customers. Broad generalisations can be very misleading, and the view that we only find cupboard bases in north Wales, and 'potboard' bases in the south is not quite true. Both of these main types were produced in all areas, and indeed often offered as alternatives by the same carpenters. Nevertheless, many local styles and variations are certainly discernible.

Amongst the oldest dressers we find are those made in Snow
donia in the early 18th century, invariably in a dense heavy nativ
oak, which was even used for the backboards and the insides o
drawers. Normally quite small and with overhanging tops, the
nearly always have cupboards in the base, and no two are eve
identical. Often the most expensive and sought after today, the
original homes would now be considered cottages. As time went o
dressers from north Wales tended to be larger, with a typical 1
arrangement of drawers in the base, with cupboards on each side
Gradually pine was used for some of the parts, especially in coast
districts where oak was scarce. Although many of the later example
were quite plain, some were decorated with large pieces of inla
especially on Anglesey and in parts of Caernarfonshire. Many o
these are so elaborate as to be known in the trade as 'Christma
tree' dressers! As a rule, the decoration of dressers in the north
quite understated, with a simple display of pewter or a crocke
service in blue and white, with perhaps a few Staffordshire figures

Cupboard-base dressers were also made in mid and south Wale
but most seem to have had open potboards under the drawers. Th
may initially have been to hold the crocks and tubs required
those areas where surplus dairy products were sold, and then ju
became the local fashion. This form allows more opportunities
display pottery, and is sometimes preferred today for that reaso
Some examples date from the mid 18th century, but there was co
tinuous production of this style until the late 19th century, especia
in Cardiganshire and Pembrokeshire. Many are quite elaborate, wi
fretted designs above the rack and below the drawers, and occa
sionally even inlaid patterns on the drawer-fronts, but many a
quite basic. But in south Wales particularly, they were intended
be seen covered in lustre jugs and brightly coloured plates, whe
their whole appearance becomes transformed.

Pembrokeshire is particularly associated with a type of hybri
base – the 'dog-kennel' – with an open space between two cu
boards. This took over from the potboard in many parts of we

Wales and was being produced in pine in large quantities by the beginning of the 20th century. As people acquired more knick-knacks and ornaments the racks also became partly enclosed with glass cupboards on each side. It was this basic style with glass cupboards in the top and an enclosed or partly enclosed base which became the main type used in the industrial areas, where it held the same place in the family's esteem as it had in the farmhouse of the previous centuries.

Dressers were never completely utilitarian, their display function was always important. Over the years the use to which they have been put has changed, and each new owner, whether the dresser was inherited or purchased, has interpreted it with their own personality.

FOOD CUPBOARDS & LINEN PRESSES

It was not only dressers which were used for display. Glazed cupboards which hang on the wall or stood on a cupboard base, were made to fit against the side or into corners. And the famed 'cwpwrdd tridarn' from Snowdonia had a top tier above the two cupboard sections for the display of pewter and delftware. Most cupboards however had solid doors, and were intended either for the storage of food and utensils in the kitchen, or bedding and clothing in the bedrooms. Although some designs are very general, many food cupboards are, like dressers, closely identifiable with particular areas. In Anglesey and Caernarfonshire the 'cwpwrdd bara caws' often had fretted designs in the top section for ventilation, and in Cardiganshire a distinctive form of the 'cwpwrdd deudarn' had bold gothic-shaped panels in the the top section.

The press cupboards made to hold textiles were, like the chest of Elizabeth Morris, often associated with marriages, and are found with many individual personalised details, sometimes including dates and the initials of the owner. Although found all over Wales, they

were produced on such a scale in the Teifi Valley in the later 19t
century that each home must have had several – indeed in the la:
years of the 20th century one farm in Llanfihangel-ar-arth known t
me had twelve! Some of them were for hanging clothes, with a hig
top section and only a couple of drawers below, but most hav
shelves in the top and a full chest of drawers as the base. Toda
these are perhaps not always as useful as the cupboard-on-cup
boards which were found in the kitchens. Large chests of drawe
were also a feature of most bedrooms, and even quite massiv
examples are referred to in west Wales as 'half drawers' or 'ha
chests', to distinguish them from the two-part presses and chest:
on-chests.

CHESTS AND BEDS

Closely related to the chests of drawers and presses, and also fc
holding blankets and clothing, were the large chests with lift-u
lids. Their quality is often quite exceptional, but it is not always ea:
to accommodate them in the modern home. Because of their siz
many have been consigned to the outbuildings over the year
where they were used to hold animal feed or simply left to rot. Th
most sought-after are the earlier examples, especially if they a
small and have a little carving and perhaps a date.

Despite the impressive number of items which are available
hold blankets and quilts, very few actual beds have survived. Th
majority of these would have been very simple frames, and th
elaborate, but cumbersome, cupboard beds were nearly all replace
in the late nineteenth century by what were believed to be the mo
hygienic brass and iron types. Even when old wooden exampl
survive, they are often of too irregular a size – and too claustr
phobic – for present tastes. Many homes had beds which actual
folded up in the day to be disguised as chests and sideboards, ar
they are similarly difficult to accommodate today. Most hom

would have had cradles, with high corner posts to facilitate gentle rocking, and these were handed down, with designs remaining unchanged for generations. Unfortunately, these too can be difficult to find space for now, and remain greatly undervalued.

TABLES AND CHAIRS

Perhaps the pieces which people have the most trouble finding are usable tables and chairs. Ideas of comfort and habits of eating and entertaining are quite different today, and the long table with plenty of knee-room with a large matching set of chairs which so many seek, was not really part of the traditional way of life. The main living room – the kitchen – normally had two tables. A long one was kept under the light of the window, and served as a work-surface as well as for eating. It frequently had deep drawers in the ends or on the long side, and was used with benches. The other table was small and round, usually with three legs, and was moved round as required. A 'setl' or 'sgiw' stood alongside the hearth, providing a draught-free area around the fire, and the room was full of stools and odd chairs. If there was a separate parlour – which would have doubled as a bedroom – there might be other tables with fold-out leaves which could be brought into the centre as required.

DESKS AND CLOCKS

An overview of the furniture found in the countryside cannot do justice to the many individual pieces which craftsmen produced, and much of which could actually fall into several categories. Partly due to the influence of Non-Conformity, the Welsh were among the most literate nations in Europe, and the variety of desks and bureaux produced was staggering. Closely similar in design and appearance

to linen presses, desks were often actually incorporated into these
pieces, and occasionally even into dressers. Space was always at a
premium, and many other pieces were also required to perform two
functions, as when for example settles had cupboards attached to
the back of them, or even backs which fell forward to form a table.
Clocks could also be built into other pieces, but normally they held
pride of place in their own right. The longcase clock stood alongside the dresser, and with the dresser has come to symbolise the
family home. Specialist collectors can be very disparaging about
country-made examples, which often had very simple movements
in the 18th century and were all mass-produced in Birmingham in
the 19th century. But the cases were wonderfully crafted pieces of
furniture, and remained locally made until the end. They incorporate the best of the features found on dressers and cupboards
from their area, and complement them perfectly. As with other categories of furniture, the finest examples are often from those villages
and small market towns which many people today would regard as
quite remote.

WHAT TO LOOK FOR

People have been collecting Welsh furniture for over a hundred
years and others have been busily faking it for just as long. Antique
collecting is subject to changes in fashion, and whilst some pieces
will always be desirable, features which were valued in 1900 may
not be as sought-after today. Heavy and intricate carving, for example,
was an essential part of the Victorian idea of antique oak, but is
now definitely a minority interest. At all periods, different people
look for different things. Many look for a high degree of perfection
whereas others find the appeal in a rustic well-used appearance
with a fair share of bashes and knocks. Others can be very particular
about the periods, and will not look at pieces made after 1800 or
even 1700. As more research is done into craftsmen and a great deal

of early-looking furniture is shown to be traditionally made but quite late in date, some of these people may be in for a few shocks. Others collect particular categories, such as clocks, or items with inlaid decoration, or pieces from a particular area.

The important thing to remember is that furniture was produced in Wales for people with limited means and limited space. Each piece was expected to be functional, and the requirements of the rural farmhouse or cottage were not the same as those of the modern home with its large windows, central heating, fitted carpets and built-in wardrobes and kitchens. Pieces have to be accepted for what they are, and if chairs are not as comfortable as we would like, or tables a bit too high or too low, or if a bureau won't accommodate the personal computer – then so be it. Few pieces in fact continue to serve their original function, so much has our life changed. But many can be accommodated to new usages, and linen presses for example are now used primarily as drinks cabinets (or TV cabinets if they're deep enough!). Within the limits of how a piece can now be used or given precious house-room, the features which determine the price collectors are willing to pay are the same as for most collecting fields – rarity, originality, decorative appearance, and provenance. Two pieces which appear to have the same description may vary enormously in their appeal and market value. Some types were rare right from the start. The 'cwpwrdd tridarn' was probably found in a very high percentage of homes in Snowdonia in the 17th and 18th centuries – but only in that area of scattered farmhouses. Examples have always been highly sought after across the border, and the number left in original homes is tiny. The 'coffor bach' was produced in far greater numbers, and although only in an area of similar size (west Wales), one that was much more densely populated. However, their small proportions and associations with family marriages means that people are rarely willing to part with them and they are not often offered for sale. On the other hand, some pieces which were once common have become hard to find simply because they were thrown out when no

Oak 'coffor bach', with a flowing design inlaid in holly and bog oak.
West Wales. Late 18th century.

longer required. Large plain oatmeal chests, cheese presses, and th
cupboard beds mentioned earlier are incredibly rare, but their pric
is low since they cannot easily be found house space.

The rarer a piece, the less important it might be if there hav
been restorations over the years. Some alterations, if done durin
the working life of a piece, can be quite an attraction, but there ar
limits. A 'coffor bach' with a new lid *and* new drawers *and* new fee
would need to be very special in some other way to have muc
value. One aspect which alterations invariably interfere with is th
desirability of an original surface finish – the patination that come
from years of polishing and exposure to the atmosphere. Piece
which have had extensive additions or been over-zealously cleane

own will never have the same appearance, and their appeal will wear off as quickly as their quick-fix polish.

One of the great distinguishing features of our furniture is its colour. Most pieces were made of locally grown timber, and depending on the soil and aspect, the colour varies. It also often varies between different parts of the finished piece, according to its treatment over the years. To worry about achieving a close match between your various pieces, or to accept something which has been substantially re-finished, is to miss out on one of the greatest virtues of Welsh furniture. Although oak in particular is very difficult to work, the craftsmen always produced a very fine finish, and the high polish which this surface has received over the years is easily maintained but difficult to re-create.

Whilst some quite primitive tables and chairs rely on their sheer simplicity for effect, in general minor decorative details greatly add to the desirability of a piece. Apparently small features can make a big difference. Dressers with shaped racks, rows of spice drawers, and elaborate aprons under the drawers will be double the price of plainer examples. And styles which are unpopular, such as large chests, are suddenly valued if they are decorated with inlaid designs or unusual panelling.

PROVENANCE AND PERIOD

Provenance is a much more esoteric quality, and refers to the known history and associations of an item. It does not necessarily interest everyone, but it can be nice to think that something has stood in the same location for generations, or that it has been in the collection of someone known to be an authority. It can be even better if it is associated with somebody who is important nationally, locally, or perhaps just to you and your family. The appeal of sitting at a table which has been used by someone with whom you can identify is a personal one, and cannot be easily translated into monetary terms.

Ash stick chair with a shaped comb-back, of a style
probably made by a wheelwright.
West Wales. Late 18th century.

Plenty of information is available about the sequence of style
and methods of construction by which we try to establish dates c
manufacture. For Welsh furniture, however, much of this needs t
be taken with a pinch of salt. Craftsmen worked within the
abilities and the wishes of their customers, and were not necessaril
particularly interested in the fashions of far-off towns. Tradition;
styles and especially time-honoured skills were highly valued, an
each piece was made to last and to be handed down, not to b

dispensed with as each new style came along. So a press cupboard with pegged joints and shaped bracket feet which looks as if it should be given a date of 1780, might actually have been made in 1840. It is far more important to buy something which suits your needs and which you find attractive, than to worry about the exact date.

Dealers and collectors operate within an agreed and rather artificial convention for dating. This is based on the received wisdom of when a style was in vogue in urban areas, with time added on to take account of various factors. A small number of dates are used, and while they give a good idea of the general sequence of styles, they are not necessarily very accurate. If you looked at too many price labels you might imagine that Welsh craftsmen worked like madmen in 1780, producing absolutely vast quantities. Fortunately, they seem to be seen to take a well-deserved break until the next feverish burst in 1800!

FAKES AND ALTERATIONS

In the end, what attracts you and what you find acceptable, is a matter of taste and pocket. The market which determines relative values may have got it quite wrong as far as you are concerned – so ignore the crowd and collect something which others overlook. But one thing that should not be acceptable is the passing off of fakes and significant alterations as the real thing. Unfortunately, if people want something and the price rises enough, others will always step in and fill the demand. In 1900 antiques dealers in west Wales collected plain chests and enthusiastically chipped away to satisfy the yearning in London for original Welsh 16th and 17th century carving. These pieces are still around, and having acquired a century of polishing, re-emerge from time to time. And today people turn large chests of drawers into small bureaux, chests with lift-up lids into cupboards, and short tables with pine tops into long tables with oak tops. Plain dressers somehow become elaborate dressers and even the smashed-up remnants of part of a dresser can become an elaborate dresser! Be cautious if you are offered something very desirable at a low price, and remember that you have to be extre mely lucky to find a bargain – there is always someone more knowledgeable one step ahead who would have snapped it up first Of course, many fakes are not even given the benefit of cheapness and a high price is no guarantee of authenticity.

Any significant purchase should always be accompanied by a detailed receipt with a description and a list of restoration. You should know what the price includes, since any additional commission and costs of storage and transport can be significant, especially with furniture. Welsh carpenters did us a great favour in that respect - most of the larger pieces split into two or even three. The solid and heavy cupboards and dressers had to be transported many mile from the workshop over muddy and stony tracks by horse or, if they were fortunate, by horse and cart. And as the family grew and then shrank over time, it may often have moved again. In the 20th cen tury a vast quantity of Welsh furniture moved very great distance indeed, to London, the Continent and America, but as interest develop at home this period is hopefully nearing an end.

THE WELSH QUILT

Jen Jones

A QUILT, BY DEFINITION, consists of two pieces of fabric placed either side of a layer of wadding and then stitched together. The best Welsh quilts, in my opinion, surpass all others in the variety and ingenuity of the stitching patterns used to join these three layers. A typical Welsh quilt is most commonly a wholecloth quilt (made from two solid pieces of cloth, either floral or plain) rather than a patchwork where a variety of fabrics are pieced together before the quilting process. A representative Welsh quilt has a large central motif (usually circular with in-fill) surrounded by various patterns (leaves, swirls, fans, hearts, diamonds, etc.) working their way outwards towards a border which sometimes repeats the inner designs in miniature or can introduce an entirely new motif. They were always made on a frame consisting of two long poles and two shorter flat pieces of wood which slotted into them to form a rectangle which could be adjusted as the quilt progressed.

Artistry in the stitching patterns is what distinguishes a Welsh quilt from, say, an American one, which relies almost entirely on a series of patchwork designs that tell their own stories. For instance, the wedding ring design in patchwork might have been used as one of the quilts in an American girl's 'hope-chest': this is not to say that the Welsh did not produce wonderful and surprising patchworks or that some American quilts are not quilted magnificently. It is a generalisation which helps to define the typical quilt from each country.

The Welsh quilt is often confused with the North Country English

(Durham) quilts because they, too, produced numerous wholecloth quilts. A trained eye differentiates between them immediately through the distinctive patterning. For me the Welsh quilt is like a framed picture whereas the North Country ones are more like wallpaper - flowing in their designs and less contained. A North Country quilt was always padded with a thin layer of cotton batting whereas the best Welsh ones were generously filled with carded fleece.

Although quilting in Wales existed in the seventeenth and eighteenth centuries, it was the province of the wealthy. Fabrics were dear and not easily afforded by the poorer classes who relied on homespun woollen blankets for their bedding. It was not until cheaper roller printed fabrics were available (c.1840) that the wholecloth Welsh quilt began to be produced in any numbers. The bulk of Welsh quilting was produced during a relatively short time – mid 19th century to the outbreak of World War II.

The cosy notion of the sewing bee where the ladies of the community got together to quilt and gossip was not a Welsh concept. Sometimes quilts were made in the home by the women of the household but the vast majority were sewn by professionals. Seamstresses in the towns and villages quilted to order and the farmlands were serviced by itinerant quilters who would journey from farm to farm – usually accompanied by an apprentice. They could make a quilt in about a fortnight. Nancy Lewis, one of the better known and more skilled quilters in the Carmarthenshire area was ambidextrous and could produce, if pressed, a quilt with her apprentice in just under a week. They would be given their room and board and about £1 after which they would continue on to the next farm to repeat the process. The housewife or farmer's wife always supplied the fabric and filling and very often, in the case of the itinerants, a frame would be part of the farm's standard equipment.

Because of the utilitarian nature of the Welsh quilt it is even more astounding to find such amazing variety amongst them. Without consciously trying to produce anything more than a bed cover the Welsh quilters were enormously creative and produced astounding

ariations within their work. Flannel wholecloth and flannel pieced
uilts with bold and original designs were often created, particularly
n the farms. These, beautiful as they were, were not highly valued
nd often relegated to lofts and sheds by the following generations
where they became prime targets for the moth. Even worse – they
ere popular as tractor covers or as lagging for hot water tanks.
bout ten years ago I was buying several very pretty floral quilts
om two elderly sisters in Llanrhystud. I asked them if they had
ver had any of the flannel quilts which I prize so highly. After a
hort whispered interchange between the two, they took me into
eir bedroom and asked me to help them lift the mattress from an
normous double bed. There, lying between it and the box spring
as a marvellous Central Star red, blue and black flannel quilt still,
ank heavens, in very fine condition. It is now one of the favourites
n my collection. Wholecloth cotton in plain colours and wholecloth
owered and patterned cottons were very popular. In fact, the
ajority of the quilts made between 1880 and 1940 were in this
tegory. Strippy, military and tailors' sample quilts were numerous.
otton patchworks and printed patchwork fabric quilts were
entiful. A certain number of appliqué and embroidered quilts
uld also be found. Quilts ranged in quality from the finest satin
otton filled with lambs-wool and stitched with intricate detail to the
timate 'thrifty' quilt – one that had worn out and been recovered –
erhaps even more than once. In between you had those filled with
otton batting or old threadbare strips of blanket and sometimes
en a combination of blankets, wool and derelict clothing.

They were all made to be used. They were utilitarian: even the
owry quilts (half a dozen being standard for a prospective bride's
ottom draw). Some were put away for best which accounts for the
ct that some of the quilts appearing today are a hundred years
d in mint condition and have hardly ever been on a bed. More
an likely they would only have been brought out when visitors
ere due or the doctor was calling to see a sick member of the
mily. One lady in Capel Dewi sold me a lovely floral quilt which

Photo: Jen Jones

A chintz quilt around a central motif. Swansea, 1840.

she remembered hiding under as a small child, when she was ailir
with the mumps and Dr John was on his way.

As I have already stated, quilting was not a self-conscious sou
searching endeavour in Wales. It was an occupation. A woman i
Wales had few avenues open to her in terms of employment; sh
could be a domestic which usually meant leaving her home town c
village; become a prostitute; or sew. It was a means by which
Welsh woman could supplement the family's income or, in mar
cases, support her children if she had been widowed or herself
she had never married. A certain Megan Jones, a spinster from th

landeilo area, was renowned for her needlework and quilting. She sewed from morning until night stopping only for a bowl of *cawl* at midday. She suffered from intense migraines but did not allow them to deter her from her task. Instead she wound a large handkerchief round her head, bound it tightly and went on with her stitching. She continued in this vain until she was 65 when she met an elderly widower. They were married shortly thereafter and she never picked up her needle again!

Unfortunately, the financial return for the time involved became less viable and by the turn of the century, unhappily, Welsh quilting was on the wane. Following the 1914-18 War, there was a further noticeable decline. Massed produced coverlets, white counterpanes (including the marcellas), tapestry bedspreads and eiderdowns consumed a large portion of the market. Another factor contributing to the decline of the hand sewn quilt was the exodus of young women from towns and villages to work for the war effort. They no longer had the time to master the techniques or were willing to train to do something so time-consuming yet non-remunerative.

Between the wars there was a resurgence of quilting which owed itself, to a lesser extent, to the efforts of the amateur WI quilters and, to a greater extent, to a scheme established by the Rural Industries Bureau in 1928. The purpose of this scheme was to stimulate craft industries in parts of Wales where the depression was taking its toll. The more expert rural quilters, particularly those in the valleys, were encouraged to perfect their techniques and refine their workmanship. They were financially assisted in obtaining the finest fabric and filling and Cardiff and London outlets were found for their quilts, primarily through commercial galleries. The quilts produced during this time were some of the finest ever to be made in Wales. The standard had to be of the highest. The quilts (and pillow shams) were to adorn the beds of the best hotels; Claridges, The Dorchester, Grosvenor House. Many were purchased by the aristocracy and even by the Royals. How far this resurgence would have progressed one can only speculate. Sadly, with the outbreak of World

War II it all ground to a resounding halt. Attempts at revival after th
war, particularly a conference in 1950 at the newly founded Wels.
Folk Museum (St Fagan's) resulting in a competition and exhibitio:
the next year, enjoyed limited success.

The current 'revival' spearheaded by the enthusiastic America:
traditionalists and by the Quilters Guild has produced some fin
quilts but they are mainly patchwork – not typical Welsh wholeclot.
and the numbers are minuscule compared to the thousands upo.
thousands produced in the heyday of this most exciting and colou:
ful of Welsh crafts. The real Welsh quilt is now a finite commodity.
is a part of the Welsh heritage. Until recently it was barely recog
nised as such and certainly not accorded the respect it was due
Happily, today, it is not only those from abroad who appreciate th
Welsh quilt. The Welsh people themselves are beginning to valu
what had very nearly been lost to them. The current generation sav
their mothers and grandmothers cover sick cows or frost endangere
potato beds with them, or worse yet, throw their old quilts on th
bonfire. Luckily the young women of today are now eager to own
Welsh quilt and thus purchase a piece of Welsh history which the
will treasure and preserve.

twrio

Welcome to the world of antiques, particularly those things made in Wales and those of interest to the Welsh collector. You may be a serious collector or merely take an interest in those items left here from our past. In either case you will find something to interest you.

Each chapter has been written by an acknowledged expert in their field, from porcelai... furniture, from courtship to quilts, commemorative pottery to samplers and maps. You read about porcelain made in Wales for the houses of the rich in London, or the potter... and vernacular furniture destined for humbler dwellings in their own locality. All are n... collected both in Wales and further afield.

The S4C television series has prese... a wide selection of interesting mat... to the Welsh-speaking inhabitants... the Principality and this book give... those of us who are less fortunate... opportunity to share the Twrio experience. The information glean... from around Wales has kindled the... enthusiasm of the audience for ou... heritage, as have the items sold on... programme.

We hope that by reading this book... you will discover a little more abo... our Welsh history and possibly der... much enjoyment from collecting s... of these antiques for yourself.

£7.99

Cover photograph: Copyright © Richard Bebb, Country Antiques (Wales)
Cover design: Derryl Rees

TOWY PUBLISHING

S4C

ISBN 0-952579-02